"I thought this would be a se[...] and oh so wrong. Funny, rela[...] brings levity to this weighty conversation. Do yourself a favor and do not skip the marginal notes. My eyes happily skipped to the side of the page every time I saw one!

"Invite your mom friends to buy this book, then discuss it over coffee, even if you have to ignore the piled-up laundry or finally clear the dining room table to have them over."

Anna LeBaron, author of *The Polygamist's Daughter: A Memoir*

"*Missionary Mom* serves as both a rallying cry and a battle plan in the fight for our children. Packed with practical advice, woven with Scripture, and seasoned with belly laugh–inducing humor, this book is a delight to read. And yet it is so much more than an easy read. It is a foundational book for those who have the noble task of raising children, influencing children, or simply living on a planet full of children. This is a book I will recommend and refer to often in the years to come. I am so grateful for this invaluable resource."

Jennifer Marshall Bleakley, author of *Joey: How a Blind Rescue Horse Helped Others Learn to See*

"If you are looking for an engaging and intensely practical guide to what on earth you're supposed to do to raise kids who love one another and God, this is the book for you. I have watched Shontell walk this out and I am changed as a result."

Emily Thomas, host of the *Mom Struggling Well* podcast

"As moms, we sometimes feel as if our daily work of mothering is rather mundane and lacking in importance. Nothing could be further from the truth, however. As Shontell so beautifully points out, motherhood is actually one of our greatest mission fields. What I especially love is that she doesn't merely leave us with that lovely concept—she also provides us with truly practical ideas, wisdom, and inspiration (and let's face it, a great sense of humor!) for how to go about being intentional missionaries as moms. We have the tools at our disposal, and Shontell teaches us how to use them. I highly recommend this book!"

Rebekah Hargraves, blogger and host of the
Home and Hearth podcast

"No matter how you slice it, parenting is hard. So often we feel unqualified, certain we're falling short and doing it all wrong. But in the pages of this book, I've found encouragement to parent my kids regardless of my imperfections and misguided attempts. Brewer reminds us that 'nothing you do will screw up your kids so much that God cannot intervene.' This is the kind of freedom every mom needs. It reminds us that he is capable of our impossible. This is the best parenting book I've read in a long time, and a resource I will keep within reach."

Carey Scott, author of *Unafraid: Be You, Be Authentic,
Find the Grit and Grace to Shine*

Missionary
MOM

Embracing the Mission Field
Right Under Your Roof

SHONTELL
BREWER

Kregel
Publications

Missionary Mom: Embracing the Mission Field Right Under Your Roof
© 2018 by Shontell Brewer

Published by Kregel Publications, a division of Kregel Inc., 2450 Oak Industrial Dr. NE, Grand Rapids, MI 49505.

ISBN 978-0-8254-4538-5

Printed in the United States of America
18 19 20 21 22 23 24 25 26 27 / 5 4 3 2 1

Dedicated to HH Brewer.
Thank you for raising babies with me.

Contents

Acknowledgments

$\mathcal{M}$y village of mamas: Mel, Erin, Marie, Newbs, Jess, and Joelle. My kids would be different humans without you.

Chris and Morgan Lienhard: My kids would be different humans without you.

My mama: Thank you for giving me Jesus and showing me that I have more than I realize.

Jessica Kirkland: Thanks. For all of this.

1

What Is a Missionary Mom?

Jesus came and told his disciples, "I have been given all authority in heaven and on earth. Therefore, go and make disciples of all the nations, baptizing them in the name of the Father and the Son and the Holy Spirit. Teach these new disciples to obey all the commands I have given you. And be sure of this: I am with you always, even to the end of the age."
—MATTHEW 28:18–20

I hate how easily guilt sets in for me. I heap it on myself and don't intentionally blame others. But every time I am at church and the missionaries are talking about upcoming trips and sharing pictures of their recent journeys, or our pastor is talking about how each of us can make a difference on a mission team, I feel like a bucket of guilt has been dumped on my head. In my vision of it all, the guilt is in the form of green slime, and it takes forever to ooze down to my toes—just as, I am sure, the devil intends.

After years of helping my brother pack for mission trips, donating money to friends to help them fund their outreaches, and listening to countless tales of my own mother's life changing experiences, I just *knew* I should join them in the field. I decided to talk to my husband about it right after church.

Seriously, even my mother? How could she?

Fired up to serve, I looked down and beheld my five little children seated quietly in their chairs and tried to picture them sleeping in a floorless hut, taking their gigantic pills for who-knows-what disease, and sharing Jesus by way of large hand gestures because, of course, we don't speak anything other than English. At that moment, I realized God was not calling me to another part of the world.

My shoulders went a little droopy with disappointment. I began feeling as if my season of mothering small children was going to be something to suffer through. You know? Until I got to the *real* work God has planned for me.

What Am I Doing Here?

Do you ever feel like you cannot remember your purpose? I mean, maybe you know some of it, but you cannot quite find that big, glowing path some of those other joy-filled mothers claim to be following. At the end of the day, you have worked a full day, washed some laundry, dried some dishes, cooked some food for people living in your house, and swept a floor. Still, you are left thinking, "That can't really be all I am meant to do, right?"

Picture Goldie Hawn after her first day of playing "mother" in the movie Overboard. Remember how the kids just kept throwing grapes at her while she mumbled, "Bub buh buub"?

Maybe you find yourself pursuing so many paths that between keeping up with your kids' hectic schedules, your husband's business dinners, and an ongoing list of ministries, you end each day staring at the wall, mouth agape, fully exhausted, and wondering what in the world you accomplished. And, please, don't get me started on giving back to the community, because most days I think showering is about as giving as I can be to others. Unless you count how many diapers I contribute to the dump each year, the number of children I have added to the earth, or how knowledgeable I am about getting lip gloss out of my favorite T-shirt once it's gone through the dryer.

Of course, after I am done with this line of thinking, I start feeling guilty for seeming so useless. Isn't our thought process relentless? Am I alone in this? One minute I am overwhelmed by my calling and the next I'm just confused by it. I have proof that I am not alone in this— all I have to do is spend a few minutes with other moms to know we all need a little clarity at times. (I've added some of their thoughts, and their kids' thoughts, throughout the book.)

Luckily, God subtly dropped a message in my brain: maybe my mission field is closer than I thought. I don't think God meant it to be so convoluted.

> **Before I was even pregnant, I knew that being a mom was my calling.** —Laura, Missionary Mom of two

No Place Like Home

If you are a mother, your purpose is clear. You may or may not be called to a foreign country, but you are certainly called to be a missionary. I repeat—you *are* called to be a missionary.

Take a minute and look around. What do you see? *Who* do you see? My friend, you are looking at your mission field. Your mission field is your home, and your mission is to share Jesus with those little people who call you Mommy.

Think about it: If you don't teach your kids to live for God, who will? Their teachers? Maybe, but not likely. Their Sunday school leaders? I suppose they add something, but you cannot reasonably expect your kids to become the men and women God intends by having them sit through an hour of lessons and icebreaker games on Sunday. The neighbors? It could happen—I pray it happens—but many times my son comes home sharing the special words the neighbors taught him, and they never sound like descriptors of God.

"Mama, what is a lazy layabout?"

"Um, why?"

"Ava's mom said her dad is a lazy layabout and he only works hard at baseball and beer."

Let's agree that we can't leave this to chance.

In fact, much of the responsibility of teaching children to live fully for Christ falls on the parents' shoulders. So, now you can stop wondering and start doing! *But wait, what do I do?* (I can almost hear you.) You begin your mission where God has you.

Right here.

Right now.

With these people.

(See me pointing?)

> Your mission field is the place where you live right now—
> the children you have right now,
> the husband you have right now,
> the home you have right now,
> the friends and neighbors you have right now,
> the body you have right now,
> the widows and orphans you know right now,
> the church members you see right now,
> and the job you have right now, even if you hate it.

Why do I feel like one of the Goonies down in the well? "Down here, it's our time. It's our time down here. That's all over the second we ride up Troy's bucket."

Don't get caught up with where you will be tomorrow.

Be purposeful *right now*.

Missionary work is not for the faint of heart. We have a calling. Moms, we are called to the mission field.

A missionary . . .	A godly mother . . .
Lives to love God and others.	Lives to love her children.
Is eager for everyone she meets to know God truly and personally.	Wants most for her children to know God.
Is teachable and willing to teach.	Teaches her children everything she can to make them as wise as possible.
Puts others first and is willing to look at the world through another's eyes.	Puts her children's needs over her own, often, to allow for as much snuggling as possible.
Is willing to learn a foreign language.	Can interpret Baby Talk, Teenage Gibberish, and the ever-confusing Subtly Rude Body Language.
Does not always get to follow the path she wants but is willing to follow the path God puts before her.	Is willing to follow after God's plan.
Is willing to sacrifice sleep, comfort, time, and toilets for the tiny chance of making the difference of heaven or hell in a person's life.	Pretty much has no choice but to sacrifice sleep, comfort, time, and toilets for the sake of raising children.
Leaves a legacy.	Leaves a legacy.

Does this sound like the kind of mom you want to be? Sound like any moms you know? Uh, hello. I think you're getting my point. These are some very clear ways a missionary and a godly mom converge to become a *Missionary Mom*.

Your Legacy Lived Out

As we step further into our role as Missionary Moms, we see evidence of change in our children as they grow and make bigger and more meaningful life choices. We see it in the way our kids chase Jesus down their own path and in their own way. And we see change in ourselves as all we've been working toward moves from words on a page to our legacy lived out. A missionary is only as effective as the legacy she leaves behind. Your legacy is reflected in your everyday choices to love in the small ways.

Jesus named one woman who lived like this. One woman whose legacy would be "preached throughout the world." And "what she has done will also be told, in memory of her" (Mark 14:9 NIV). Jesus said that.

Jesus. God, made in flesh, pointed out this woman who once sat at his feet while her sister cooked up a storm in the kitchen and passive-aggressively called her lazy (Luke 10:38–42). This same woman who told Jesus she knew her brother Lazarus would still be living if Jesus had arrived earlier (John 11:32). Mary of Bethany chose to love Jesus at any cost, and he honored her for it with a promise (Mark 14).

Picture it.

Less than a week before the Passover and the Feast of Unleavened Bread, Jesus has finished dinner at the house of Simon the Leper. The disciples are there, lounging around the table. Jesus is reclining a few pillows over as Mary enters holding an incredibly expensive bottle of perfume. She cracks the top and pours the contents out over Jesus's hair and ends by rubbing the perfume on his feet in a foreshadowing of Jesus washing the disciples' feet—the ultimate service to a person in that day.

"Why this waste of perfume?" (Mark 14:4 NIV). Conversation breaks out in mumbles across the room, started by none other than Judas Iscariot. He is offended. He's mostly concerned with the fact that he now has to miss out on his piece of the pie (or perfume) because if this oil is used to honor Jesus, Judas cannot sell it and pretend to give that money to the poor. He is indignant.

"'It could have been sold for a year's wages and the money given to the poor!' So they scolded her harshly" (Mark 14:5).

Jesus knows Judas's heart, but more importantly, he knows Mary's heart. She is more focused on making her moments with Jesus count than she is with helping the poor right now. She focuses on showing Jesus she adores him; she is not focused on the snide remarks seeping from the group of men at the end of the dinner table.

Maybe she knows these same guys were recently reprimanded for begging to be Jesus's right-hand men because of their misguided self-worth. Maybe she simply does not care. She does not need to defend herself. Jesus speaks up, "Leave her alone. . . . She has done what she could" (Mark 14:6, 8).

He doesn't list her accolades or talk about the hardships she has recently experienced. And there were many. He says, "She did what she could."

Do What You Can

I don't know about you, but I want my Savior to say of me, "She did what she could." Too many days go by when I lay my head on my pillow, and I cannot honestly say I did what I could.

I could have.

I should have.

But, most days, I choose not to.

Did I just admit that? This is why Mary's legacy reads, "Wherever the Good News is preached throughout the world, this woman's deed will be remembered and discussed" (Mark 14:9).

Wherever the gospel is preached! Isn't that pretty much *every*where? Everyone everywhere will know that "she did what she could." I don't need that level of recognition, but I sure do want this phrase to come to Jesus's mind when we meet face to face for the first time. When my children think of me. When my husband considers the job I did as a wife and mother. This will not occur by happenstance. I have to choose my priorities and, like the Scripture says, do what I can.

Chances are, you are a mom like the rest of us: hectic, harried, and probably hairier than you would like to be because you don't have time to take care of that regularly. Chances are, you are a mother like Mary of Bethany who has company to cook for and some family drama and a sister who thinks you could be doing better and isn't afraid to tell you so. The difference I see between women of our generation and those of Mary's day is how willing those first-century women were to stop whatever they were doing and handle what was important. We, in contrast, are typically too busy to even notice there is something to deal with.

We aren't told whether Mary knew her time with Jesus was limited. She probably didn't know Jesus was about to be handed over to the Jewish Pharisees, but she was not a girl who put things off for tomorrow. She did what she could *when* she could. One commentary said, "If she had not done it now, she could not have done it at all."[1]

Missing the chance to love like this feels like a punch in my gut. I don't want to miss windows of opportunity. I want to live like Mary of Bethany and say with confidence that I did what I could *when* I could. Our mission field awaits. Let's do what we can, right now.

Who knows, maybe you really will end up traveling across the globe as part of your missionary journey. Nevertheless, for now, God may be calling you to be a Missionary Mom.

2

What Can We Do, What Can't We Do?

You know everything I do.
You know what I am going to say
even before I say it, LORD.
You go before me and follow me.
You place your hand of blessing on my head.
Such knowledge is too wonderful for me,
too great for me to understand!
—PSALM 139:3–6

The famous poet, Robert Burns, so wisely quipped that "The best-laid schemes o' mice an' men gang aft agley."[2] And since we've already established that my foreign language skills aren't everything they could be, for everyone's benefit, this roughly translates to, "The best-laid plans of mice and men often go awry." We can pray and prep and work to be as capable as possible and still run smack-dab into the enemy's plan, face planting at his feet.

John 10 made clear the enemy's evil intentions: to kill dreams, hopes, relationships, and people themselves.

Kill.

"The thief's purpose is to steal and kill and destroy. My purpose is to give them a rich and satisfying life" (John 10:10).

Only *sometimes* is this metaphorical.

He comes to destroy our self-image and plant aggressively sprouting doubt:

What if I screw up my kids?

What if I am too late?

What if my kids make the same mistakes I made?

Two lines of reasoning spring out of these desperate questions.

1st, what *if*? So *what*? So what if you take part in a worldwide experiment to find the worst parent and you win by a landslide? What *if* your kids are already teenagers and have more than the average share of issues? What *if* your kids make the same mistakes you did?

By no means do I view these as small problems for parents to face. These problems are, however, easy for God. The end. And thank you for reading my book. Just kidding. There's more, I promise. Keep reading.

You may be familiar with Jeremiah 29:11, which reads, "'I know the plans I have for you,' says the LORD, 'They are plans for good and not for disaster, to give you a future and a hope.'" This verse is thrown about so much in church that it's almost become meaningless. One morning I was reading this passage, and it struck me that my focus was all wrong. I chewed on it a bit to fully understand God's promise in this verse. I reread it several times, emphasizing different words, and then it hit me.

I was so fixated on the part I wanted to know: the plans. I thought, "God knows *the plans*." Then I would mumble a little prayer of, "God, please tell me your plans. I need to know said plans. I prefer to know all the plans. You have made me a planner, Lord. Lord? *Lord!* Of course you want me to know what the plans are—right?" Say this last part meekly because we all know this thinking is wrong.

Of course God has *plans*, but he helped me see more to this promise. While my emphasis was on the plan, he was showing me that *he* knows.

He. *Knows.*

God knows.

He wants you only to know that *he* knows. The end— *Sometimes simply repeating things makes me laugh.*
thank you for reading my book. No, really, there is more.

Wrapped up in these words, God is saying something that sounds an awful lot like, "You don't have to fret; you do not need to spend endless nights tossing and turning over questions that never cease. No good comes of it."

God knows.

He is capable of doing our impossible, and God alone holds our children in his hands.

Look down at your hands right now. What can you accomplish with that pair? When I look at my hands, I see scars from every Thanksgiving I have attempted to make a turkey. I see creases and imperfections. I see hangnails and the remnants of nail polish I applied at least a month ago. I see that my tall finger is freakishly long. I see hands that are small and unable even to open pickle and jelly jars.

If I'm being honest, I know my hands without God to steady them are insignificant and incapable. In stark contrast, God's immense hands engulf the whole world as if it were a teeny, tiny dust mote: earth, space, stars, land, water, solar systems we don't know of, people, you, me, and our children. He holds it all willingly and perfectly, and nothing the enemy has planned can change that.

We can shelter our kids, attempting to control their every move, forcing them away from paths that seem to mirror our past blunders. The fact is, *nothing* I do as a parent can remove my child from God's hand. Nothing. *Nothing.* Nothing! My hands simply are not that big.

The book of Isaiah is full of promises reminding us that God's hands are mighty. Chapter 43 delivers a certainty with which even the devil cannot interfere. Verse 11 reads, "I, yes I, am the LORD, and there is no other Savior." Follow this truth with verse 13: "From

We do not save our kids. Our faith is our faith. Their faith is their choice.

eternity to eternity I am God. No one can snatch anyone out of my hand. No one can undo what I have done."

I sort of feel like God is saying, "I am capable. I got this. High-five."

A high five solidifies everything, don't you think?

By frantically attempting to clutch my children in my own grip, I am comparing my hands to God's hands. We have established that my hands can scarcely make a celebration turkey without injury, so this Scripture (and my turkey reputation) prove with finality that nothing I do compares to what God can and will do for my children.

- Nothing you do will screw up your kids so much that God cannot intervene.
- No fear exists that is too scary for God's hands.
- We serve a God of peace who gives new mercies every morning.

If you are going to have a ceaseless stream of dialogue at night, maybe replace those nagging, life-stealing questions with these trustworthy promises instead. Imagine the power shift. How differently will you feel in the morning after declaring God's awesomeness repeatedly through the night? You may just have a hopeful disposition when you wake.

2nd, we've established that we aren't the worst parents and that it wouldn't matter if we were. The second line of reasoning is one we can use against the doubt the enemy viciously plants in our minds, and it can be summed up in a single word.

Hope.

That is it. Four letters make up one great big word: hope.

I can have hope for my children's future because God says so, and I am not a useless, worthless human existing to get by and teach my children merely to get by. While my hands may not be called to hold the whole world, they do have a purpose. I have established what I cannot do. Let's look at what the Bible says I *can* do.

What I cannot do is not limited to turkeys, by the way. While I do not have room enough to include a thorough list of my shortcomings, I will say I cannot have small hair, stand with my eyes closed without swaying, eat pork without serious repercussions, or hear high tones in my right ear or low tones in my left ear. Let's just agree to say I have issues.

What Can We Do?

Philippians 4:13 reminds us that we "can do everything through Christ, who gives me strength." Paul, the writer of Philippians, goes on to tell us that we can be "certain that God, who began the good work within you, will continue his work until it is finally finished on the day when Christ Jesus returns" (Phil. 1:6). In case you are unsure, let me make this clear.

God has called you to mother your children. Your children are a good work God began in you the day they were conceived. *You* are who James is addressing when he mentions caring for others. You can be an amazing mother because God is holding you and your children in his very capable hands. You have what it takes to be this mother because you have God.

With our confidence in God, we can now move forward in being this new and possibly improved mother. Proverbs 3:5–6 says, "Trust in the LORD with all your heart; do not depend on your own understanding. Seek his will in all you do, and he will show you which path to take." He doesn't mean our paths will be smooth or worry free. This verse is saying we will know where and when and how and how far to walk.

Hello, Kettle;
this is Pot.
Nice to meet
you. I overplan
everything.
#planningismyjam

One obvious message in this Scripture is to trust God with our kids. The next message says stop trying to overplan for every *what if* that will come into our kids' lives in order to be ready for every possible scenario. It will never work; you will never be ready for every possible scenario. Let the dream go, woman. "Seek his will in all you do, and he will show you which path to take." This is where our role goes from incapable to imperative.

Mothers, we have the ability, privilege, and responsibility to pray for our children *daily*. Every morning, every night, every time those sweet or sour faces pop into our minds, we can take the time to say a prayer for our babies. Be bold. Be audacious. Be specific. Pray for your children.

When it comes to our kids' salvation, there is no room for vague sentiments and watery prayers. Rather than saying, "Lord, be with my son today," say, "Lord, what a blessing little Joe is to our family. Give him a thirst to know your Word so he can bring you glory from this day all the way through his life. Cause Scriptures to stick in his brain so he is ready with the best weapons when the fight lands on the doorstep of his heart." Because guess what: God already promised he would be with us and never leave us. We do not actually need to keep asking for that any more. He isn't going anywhere.

We do this often, actually—pray about things God has already handled. It's like we are coming to God repeating his ideas back to him as if they are our own.

More
prayer
talk to
come in
chapter 6.

God: I will never leave you nor forsake you.

Me: Hey, God. How about if you never leave me nor forsake me? How does that sound?

God: Uh—good. Are you just repeating what I am saying?

Me: Are *you* just repeating what *I* am saying?

This could go on forever. It seems to. We can add meaning where white-noise prayers used to exist.

Rather than saying, "Lord, protect my kid today," say, "God, you are so faithful to be the author and finisher of my child's day. Let every move he makes be toward your will for him and worthy of the gospel of Jesus Christ. Make his path clear. Open his eyes to the devil's schemes, so little Abe can recognize them for what they are: distractions and evil paths. Today, whisper in his ear the way he should go, the words he should speak, and the people he should help."

Because guess what? The Psalms remind us that God alone keeps us safe. "You alone, LORD, make me dwell in safety" (Ps. 4:8 NIV).

Be specific. Keep in mind these three areas when praying for your kids: future, present, and past. And, as you pray, do so as if you are raising a world changer.

Could This Be Your Child?

Most of us are familiar with the popular line from the story of Esther, "Who knows but that you have come to your royal position for such a time as this?" (Esther 4:14 NIV). To me, the most miraculous part about this line is the speaker. Esther was an orphan, separated from her immediate family, as were many Jews during the rule of King Xerxes. She was raised by her adult cousin, Mordecai, who treated her as a daughter. I just think that for a guy who is not biologically a father to this girl, he sure seems to fully grasp what it means to guide his child to follow God's calling, no matter the cost.

When King Xerxes basically fired his queen after a poorly thought-out tantrum, he found he needed a replacement. Xerxes instructed his men to scour the land and bring him the most eligible virgins. With a harem full of possibilities, the king's servants worked with the women, putting them through beautification treatments and teaching them manners befitting royalty. A year's worth of oiling and lotioning, lotioning and oiling.

That poor kid from The Sandlot would have really lost it!

Each girl had her chance to spend time dazzling the king, each vying for his attention and the throne. In the end, of course, he chose Esther because God's will is demonstrated even in unbelievers such as King Xerxes.

As a side story, there is royal drama between Esther's cousin Mordecai and the king's right-hand man. Ole Haman hates Jews, all of them. He's plotting to kill them mostly because of his hatred toward Mordecai. Apparently, Esther occupies the power seat: she is asked to appeal to Xerxes to save not only Mordecai but all of the Jews in 127 provinces.

Esther's initial response is not that of a queen; she has never appeared so childlike, which makes sense. While we don't know Esther's exact age, the culture and customs lead us to believe she was in her midteens when she was taken from her home, and her palace training would have taken a few years. According to several biblical timelines,[3] this puts Esther at around twenty—a child by many standards. So Esther's parent steps in—her cousin and adoptive father but also her subordinate. She is Mordecai's "adopted" daughter, but she is also his queen, and he is her husband's servant. Mordecai challenges her to be the woman she is capable of being in God's great name. Then he commits to pray for her. And he asks Esther that fateful question that changes the course of an entire people: "Who knows but that you have been chosen for such a time as this?"

> Truthfully, I don't know if I am fully equipped to be a great mother or not. I had a wonderful example to imitate, but I have a feeling my daughter is much different than I was. So far, so good, and I plan to continue to take it one day at a time.
> —Lauren, Missionary Mom of one

Do we do that with our kids? Do we ask the challenging questions? Do we lay bare the harsh truths of the situation and agree to pray and fast for our kids as they make the seemingly impossible decisions placed before them? I agree that most of our children will never face saving an entire nation. I recognize that most crossroads will not lead to bodily death on one side and salvation on the other, as Esther's crossroad did for her. But I still think every parent can benefit from this page out of Mordecai's playbook.

From a very young age, Mordecai taught Esther to obey. He took his role as her parent seriously: he advised her, he challenged her to listen to what God said, he taught her to deny herself and follow God over all others, and he prayed with her and for her. He expected much of her, and he spoke honestly with her about her future.

Somewhere along the line, Mordecai taught his young cousin the value of prayer and fasting. We know this because this is the path she took to decision-making when faced with death. Because of Mordecai's parenting, Esther respected authority, rose to the challenges before her, and sought advice from those with greater insight than her own—Mordecai and God. What a remarkable description of who we want our children to become and the steps we need to take to get them there. Your child *has* been chosen for such a time as this. What steps are you taking now to help him or her be ready?

3

Mom Guilt

Search me, O God, and know my heart;
test me and know my anxious thoughts.
Point out anything in me that offends you, and
lead me along the path of everlasting life.
—PSALM 139:23–24

$\mathcal{M}$om guilt is an ugly little lie from that reprobate we spoke of before. You know the one. He does not want you to succeed.

Steal. Kill. Destroy. Ring a bell? First Peter 5 says, "The devil . . . prowls around like a roaring lion, looking for someone to devour" (v. 8). He is like a dingo waiting for Mama to turn her back on Baby and campsite. He is just lurking in the shadows waiting for you to lower your guard. When we concede to mom guilt, we make ourselves an easy kill. Sometimes this Scripture is more literal than my heart can endure.

Mom guilt comes in so many forms it can be difficult to recognize when it appears. We allow nearly everything to make us feel as if we are doing it wrong, and then we choose one of two paths:

Who are we kidding? Mom guilt is the greatest (meanest and nastiest) lie the enemy throws our way, and I have yet to meet a mother who does not experience it.

Take to heart the list of what Junior *must* become (according to modern society), and choose every activity, every party, every opportunity to be a part of *it*—plowing through the wonder years. And, because we are exhausted, we look for a mighty escape.

Fake modern society.

Or

Compare ourselves and our list of accomplishments with other moms—the winner being the one with the busiest, saddest story. And, because we are exhausted, we look for a mighty escape.

The level of guilt we give in to varies, and so does the level of the fix: from complaining and ceaseless venting all the way to sleeping pills and more moms' nights out than moms' nights at home being moms. Escaping into the television or computer or our phones. Escaping into a glass of wine, or two or three, a night. Escaping our families to do ministry.

Yah. I said it.

It's all for naught. It is a Band-Aid. And not one that sticks for a little while so healing can take place underneath. Instead, this Band-Aid keeps the wound hidden so the devil can do his real damage, and no one is wise to his scheme.

It is all hidden, right?

And secret.

And separate.

None of these escapes leads to a peaceful, God-centered life. None equips your kid for the life God envisioned. None creates a relationship between parent and child. None creates the fellowship God spoke of in Acts 2. All of these lead to *hidden* and *separate*. These places are not God's places for you. We know this because the whole point of Jesus dying on the cross was to get rid of the separate. He died so we could have face-to-face, true, redemptive relationships.

Fellowship: Healthy and Otherwise

Think back to your child's day of birth or adoption. Good times, yes? Maybe hectic or scary at times but also so hopeful, so full of possibilities. So sweet was that little bundled baby or child! Your whole outlook changed forever. As time passed, you took the responsibility of protector seriously. Maybe too seriously, and now you refuse to give Little Girl space to breathe on her own. You are a stone's throw from packing your entire life into the minivan and heading to Appalachia because you heard about an up-and-coming commune in the wilderness with the ambition to save the coming generation from the world itself.

Or maybe you are like me—I mean, like a friend of mine—who is still offended that her fifth baby decided to be three weeks late. But whatever. I— oops—she is over it.

Be wary of communes offering protection from every evil. They may just offer you a tall glass of Flavor Aid. God sent your child to this world. He probably didn't want you to live with him or her in seclusion.

For the record, if you are going to start a cult and ask people to drink poison via flavorful sugar drink (like one infamous Jim in history, who seriously used an off-brand drink powder), go the distance and pay for the name brand, Kool-Aid. Because guess what? You are all about to die. Your savings here is slightly irrelevant. It's just a slap in the face. Also, do not start a cult.

The Bible is an excellent reference for how-to advice on healthy fellowship. We are facing this mountain together. You are not in this alone. Stop insisting you are. Stop insisting you are the only busy parent, the only struggling mom, or the only one who loves her kid enough.

Rather, speak what is good and true and upright over your family:

Hebrews 3:1: "Fix your thoughts on Jesus" (NIV).

Philippians 4:8: "Finally, brothers and sisters, whatever is true, whatever is noble, whatever is right, whatever is pure, whatever is lovely, whatever is admirable—if anything is excellent or praiseworthy— think about such things" (NIV).

Focus more on the foundational pillars God cares about, and *then* fill in your free time on your calendar. In Acts 2:42–47, we see how the people wisely spent their time:

> They devoted themselves to the apostles' teaching and to fellowship [church], to the breaking of bread and to prayer [communion, food, and prayer for one another]. Everyone was filled with awe at the many wonders and signs performed by the apostles. All the believers were together and had everything in common. They sold property and possessions to give to anyone [maybe even the sinner] who had need [serving the community and those in need and funding it by selling their nonsense and even their makes-sense]. Every day they continued to meet together in the temple courts. They broke bread in their homes [having friends and strangers over for dinner] and ate together with glad and sincere hearts, praising God [worshiping and giving God the glory for every good thing] and enjoying the favor of all the people. And the Lord added to their number daily those who were being saved. [And people loved for real, so lives were changed for real.] (NIV, bracketed notes added via the Shontell Standard Translation)

What a ministry to be a part of! They were not in their houses hiding out from the world. They were not stuck in their cars driving Junior over hill and dale for extracurricular clubs. They were not dragging a cross through populated cities, condemning the sinner. They were not standing in the middle of the local university calling

Yah, that guy denouncing tramps exists in my town. He used to be a pastor. His ministry has seriously gone downhill.

people tramps and hookers and drunks because of their clothing choices or nightly escapades. No! Instead, they devoted themselves to teaching, fellowship, eating, and prayer.

I support any ministry that shows Jesus's love through food. The end.

They went about their day looking for people who needed, and they gave as each person needed. Not simply how they wanted to give, but according to what that person *needed*.

I wholeheartedly believe not one person handed a hungry man a tract and said, "Be blessed and have a full belly, my man."

They sold anything and everything to pay for their ministry and have money to give. They did not sit back and mumble that if God wanted them to help others, then he would make the resources land in their laps. Because of this drastic lifestyle choice, God brought others to them and expanded their ministry, changing the world forever.

One More Thing on This Topic

Women! Lend me your ears! When it comes to the home, women are major example setters. Our husbands often take their cues from us when we become new parents. If we are stressed and overwhelmed at each turn, they will be as well. If we are chill and take things slow and steady, they will likely follow suit. In the same way, our children mimic our reactions to challenges, angry situations, and joyful news. And yes, there is joyful news.

I know this from personal experience because sometimes I furrow while I smile. Thanks, Mom.

First Peter 5 goes on to say, "Humble yourselves, therefore, under God's mighty hand, that he may lift you up in due time. Cast all your anxiety on him because he cares for you" (vv. 6–7 NIV). If I could just repeat this again and again until we fully grasped that statement, I would. Or you could just reread that Scripture. Look it up. Highlight it. Memorize it. Jump around. We get to cast our cares and our anxiety on God. And you thought you would never find a place for all that psychological clutter! He is asking for it. He is insisting. Because he cares for you. What do we have to do to earn that freedom and reprieve? "Humble yourselves . . ."

Look. I don't know you. I don't know how you memorize Scripture. I wanted to appeal to everyone. Perhaps you're a jumper? I don't judge.

I heard a pastor recently talk about humbling ourselves. He said we need to be willing to say, "As it happens, I don't see every part of this situation or any situation. To be frank with you, Jesus, I do not get much of what is happening, not even within my own life. I do not know myself as well as you do. I don't know my child as well as you do. My perspective is seriously minute, and I want to humble myself before you so you can be in the lead. I will follow your path and trust that you know more than I do. I do not need to be fearful. I do not need to give up. I need to cast my cares on you, and you will guide my every step. Moreover, you will take care of every corner of my life because I can't do it alone or best or even halfway right most days. You rock, Lord. Thanks for loving me anyway."

OK, maybe he said like twenty of those words, and not even in that order. But the message is pretty much right on. This pastor and Peter are both saying we need to humble ourselves before we cast our cares. We do that by realizing that we all sin and are not in control of this, that, that over there, or that thing from way back when. We do that by confessing our issues to God and accepting his forgiveness. By repenting. We do that by trusting that God has this in his hands. Ah, those really are mighty hands.

OK, Yet Another Thing

Sometimes we get caught up in how we *appear* to be mothering. From experience, we know that what we see is not always what is actually happening. We develop a mold we think the world deems acceptable, and we try to force our family into it. We go through an awful lot to appear upstanding, and probably not blatantly but somewhere deep inside, we hope people notice. Perhaps . . .

Say this next part with a dramatic voice.

The neighbors will notice us.

Our church family will give us the nod of approval.

Strangers will mimic us because our parenting is superior.

Younger mothers will quake in their newbie boots because our children are so religious.

But that's all wrong.

James 1:26–27 tells us it is not about being religious. Parenting is about caring, guiding our children, caring *for* them, teaching them, molding them, modeling *to* them, and setting up boundaries they can navigate within until they are ready to fly on their own.

Take baby birds, for example. Much care goes into the incubation period of a bird. We can compare this time to the first eighteen years we spend with our kids. Mother and father birds warm their tiny eggs and work endlessly to create an ideal nest until it is as close to perfection as possible.

Studies show that baby birds whose mothers communicated with them throughout their stay in the egg are more tolerant and well adjusted. This is also true with humans. Luckily, our "incubation" time with our kids lasts longer than the average bird, and we don't have to speak to our kids through an eggshell—although it can seem like it as they near the teen years.

Parents have years to do what that mama bird does in a couple of months. She teaches them to live well with their siblings. She teaches them to hunt and gather. She teaches them to build a nest as she continues to care for their home. Eventually she teaches them to fly. She lets them go fully, and maybe they falter a little, but typically, they spread their wings and head off to begin their own families. This process works because that mama bird knows her time is short, and she begins her work even before those baby eggs hit the nest. She doesn't sit around comparing her parenting to that of other birds.

> In general, I think being a mom means sacrificing your own immediate desires for the long-term good of your family, knowing that it is for a season, and that it's okay to want your desires back later. —Melissa, Missionary Mom of two

There is no time to spare. We begin our parenting journey staring at the coming road as if two decades is an eternity we cannot fathom ending. In reality, we need to be more like the birds in what we do:

- Preparing the way for our children by getting our hearts right
- Learning how to care for our nest from the very beginning, and creating the best nest possible so our kids have boundaries and feel secure where they live (this doesn't mean buying an expensive house and furniture; it means being a purposeful mom— allowing Christ to work in us so we have something to offer)
- Sharing Jesus with our kids from the instant they are born through prayer and example, thus equipping them with faith and right behavior as they grow
- Teaching them to love their siblings and respect authority
- Finally, giving them wings to fly and placing them in God's hands

All the time in eternity won't make a difference if we aren't arming our children with these essentials.

I Swear This Is the Last Thing

Don't feel guilty if you are following what God has called you to. Has he called you to be a working mom? Then work. Work hard, just like your Boss did (after all, he was a Jewish carpenter). Don't be manipulated by guilt for not being home to care for the house more. But then set boundaries on your other activities, because working moms do not ever become part-time mothers. You are always *the* full-time mom. And if you are called to stay home, do everything you can to keep your finances and home in order to make staying at home as doable as possible. Chances are, you have a bit more time than money. Invest that time wisely (because you've still got a Jewish carpenter for a Boss). Then release it. Don't sit around feeling guilty for not contributing to the family financially.

Whether at the office or at home, decide that you are going to compare your everyday life with who God says you are, not with the neighbor or some other mom. Choose what God says are the right priorities for your family and do them to the best of your ability. Feel assured that you are where God wants you, and then be free as a bird.

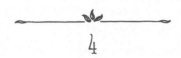

4

This Job Probably Won't Kill You: The Truth About Martyrs

I will be with you as
I was with Moses.
I will not fail you or abandon you.
—JOSHUA 1:5

$\mathcal{T}$he following is a compilation of women I have been or almost become at some point in my grown-up life. Some of the thoughts were fleeting, but they were there. I've changed my name so you won't judge me too harshly.

A Tale of Two Women

Meet Sally. Sally is a stay-at-home mom of three kids, ages three, six, and eight. She attends church with her family thirty minutes from her home because the children's church has "fun" activities for the kids and there is a MOPS (Mothers of Preschoolers) group that meets once a week. She is on two church committees except when retreat rolls around—then she is on four. Her daughter is in dance twice a week because she loves it and has a dancer's build. Her son is on a traveling baseball team because his arm is basically a Louisville Slugger attached at his shoulder. Her three-year-old participates in a neighborhood playgroup and Gymboree so he can socialize. The family spends one

Saturday a month stocking the shelves at a local food pantry, and they host a small group in their home the other three Saturdays. So she can still be involved with her school-age children, Sally volunteers in their classrooms and serves on the PTA board.

Sally is also exhausted.

She wakes up at five so she can clean or have some peaceful time in the shower. She leaves the house at seven thirty and does not typically return until it is time to make dinner. On her honest days, she admits she didn't think stay-at-home moms were gone so much. She admits she thought they stayed . . . well . . . at home. At the end of her day, she is much too tired for her husband, but she is hopeful they will get a vacation soon.

Now meet Lily. Lily is a part-time working mom of two kids: a son aged seven and a daughter aged two. She homeschools her children because she has met the kids in her neighborhood and is certain they are not the kind of people with whom her angels should socialize. She heard about a family at the school with two dads and does not want her son to be influenced by them and become homosexual. She has met some of the teachers, who admitted they celebrate Halloween in the classrooms. She read a newspaper article that confirmed her school district was taking quiet/prayer time out of the classroom, and they are considering taking God's name out of the pledge they recite each morning.

Lily arranged a job where she can work out of her home, because she wants to be the only one who raises her kids. Once she arranged for her son to have a play date with a boy next door, but he used the Lord's name in vain, so they will not be having him over again. She is convinced the world is an enemy with whom her children should have zero interaction.

Also, Lily is exhausted.

She is the only one she trusts enough to care for her children, so she never leaves them. When she is honest, she wants to hide her kids in her house and hand-select a group of people who share her identical views and live on their street. She has not had time alone in seven years. She has not had a date with her husband (without her children) since becoming a mother. Her knuckles are a permanent white from the vigilant grip she maintains to protect her children from anything not normal, biblical, or safe.

> I have been growing as a person in not feeling guilty if my house is not perfectly clean or if everything isn't in place all of the time.
> —Jessica, Missionary Mom of four

Lily and Sally met at the park, and they started chatting when their two youngest kids found each other on the slide. They talked about the weather, their husbands' jobs, and their churches. They confessed that they were sad about how fast their kids were growing. They confided that they were exhausted. Part of their conversation went something like this:

> Lily: I just want to go out with my husband. One dinner. Just one night together.
> Sally: At least you get to be home. My kids excel at so much I am a taxicab mom.
> Lily: Oh, well. I would *love* to get out of the house. But I have to do so much damage control every time we get around someone who swears or smokes or looks shady in any way. I am terrified my kids will go to hell just seeing something like that.
> Sally: I hear ya. But at least you only have two kids. Three is *so* much more work than two. That is why I am so tired. I loved having two. Two was so *easy*.
> Lily: I would never want to do everything you are doing. You

obviously do not love your kids as much as I love mine. Otherwise you would not expose them to so much evil. Your kids are probably going to be drinkers. Be careful. Extracurricular activities lead to drugs.

Sally: It has been so great spending this time with you (half smile and inner dialogue too rude to include here).

Lily: Oh *yah!* Let's do it again (half smile and inner dialogue too rude to include here).

OK, no one talks like this. Not outside of their heads. But I really think sometimes moms decide their way is the only way, no matter how warped their way becomes. They need everyone else to parent the same way. Truthfully, these women are unhappy. So many moms are unsatisfied with how they are doing it, and yet they spend their conversations trying to one-up each other's level of sacrifice as if this proves they win. They try to out-martyr the other mom.

Your circle of influence changes what comes to mind when someone mentions the word "martyr." Most of the world counts Jesus a martyr because he in fact died for his faith. He did so willingly. After Jesus, Stephen is arguably the most accredited martyr in the Bible: stoned to death by an outraged mob after he made a quick recounting of how the *current* lawmakers were a little too similar to the lame lawmakers of old (Acts 7:51–60).

Mama, Not Martyr

Dictionary.com defines a martyr as "a person who is put to death or endures great suffering on behalf of any belief, principle, or cause." We could name many biblical and modern people who fit this description. Mothers, however, are not typically among them.

Stop throwing your rotten lettuce at me. I am not saying you don't work hard or sacrifice much for a great cause. I am not one of those people who writes a "revolutionary" book on how to be the best mother possible, but once you pull back the curtain, you discover the author was actually a single man, aged fifty-five, never a dad, never a husband, bred in a Petrie dish, raised by wolves, and not at all human.

Nope.

That's me in the trenches right beside you, trying to learn how to do this the right way. I am just saying, we mothers are rarely faced with death in order to be the Missionary Moms we are called to be. Moms are called to care for and teach their kids: safety, manners, stay out of jail. Missionary Moms

Please step away from that tomato. I have a point. Hear me out.

are asked to embrace a more radical stance of raising kids. We choose to be all in for the sake of our children, not for how our children make us look to others.

Our time is short. We have eighteen Christmases. We need to bust out our Michael Jackson glove and start with the man in the mirror. Then we must alter our views enough to know that we are not the safe makers; we are the playmakers. It is time to stop being dramatic about our role and become drastic instead.

Those are D words. So is this one: Death Therapy.

What About Mom?

Take a tangent with me. In the movie *What About Bob?* Doctor Leo Marvin loses his ability to function in everyday life after acquiring a new patient, Bob Wiley. Bob drives Dr. Marvin to his breaking point after tricking his way into the good doctor's lakeside vacation home. Moreover, Bob usurps Dr. Marvin's fifteen minutes of fame when the doc chokes during

Seriously, where do you keep getting all the rotten vegetation? Don't worry. Nobody really dies. Keep reading.

his interview with *Good Morning America*. Bob is suddenly brilliant, and why shouldn't he be? He has been faking medical conditions for attention his entire adult life—he's learned a few things along the way.

Doctor Marvin sees red and drives Bob to the wilderness for a little something called Death Therapy.

Death Therapy is where you take the person with the issues and wrap them in enough explosive material to ensure they never return to interrupt your family vacation. I do not want to give away the ending of this movie, because it is a brilliance best experienced firsthand. However, I will point out that Dr. Marvin was desperate. He tried the typical channels of helping and then avoidance, but Bob's surname describes him to a T. He is wilier than a coyote. Dr. Marvin is driven to drastic measures,

I am aware that half of you are giggling, and half of you know not of what I speak. If you haven't seen this movie, do yourself a favor. Do your family a favor. Buy What About Bob? and watch it tonight. Incidentally, it's an excellent biblical lesson on loving the unlovable. Parental guidance is suggested.

and instead of sitting around feeling sorry for himself, he takes an entirely different approach to the doctor/patient relationship.

We need to have this same gumption when it comes to being Missionary Mom. Our children will continue to act and exist however they please if we do not decide our kids are high priority. We must begin parenting as if it is the greatest and biggest work we will ever do.

Extreme measures may be needed if you have tried many ways to parent and they do not seem to be working. It is Dr. Marvin's radical spirit I hope we'll mimic, not his behavior. It is the giving of 100 percent of our purpose according to God's will as parents that I hope we'll replicate. It is the "I am willing to give every ounce of myself in order for you to know God and make a far-reaching difference for his kingdom" attitude that I hope we'll glean.

Be willing, not worried.

Be ready, not forlorn.

Be aware of what could be, not devastated over how much you seem to be missing out on because you are in the season of parenting young (or old) kids.

Sometimes sighing helps.

Often I hear myself sighing heavily. Sometimes I recommend heavy sighing. One time I asked my pastor about all the sighing. He said, "Sighing helps you remember you aren't dead." He's a wordsmith, that guy. However, in reference to *this* topic, I say sigh less and gain some perspective. What we are actually experiencing in these heavy sighs is better defined as motherhood, not martyrdom.

And Now . . .

And now, a note from our Sponsor.

Dear Missionary Moms,

I did not create you to be martyrs. Your flair for the dramatic is impressive, but you are needlessly placing all the wrong pressures upon yourselves, and then you sigh deeply and ask me for energy to make it through another day. You feel guilty when you work outside of the home and can't volunteer to chaperone every field trip; you feel guilty because you loathe cleaning. I hate to say you are doing it wrong, so I will say this: You are doing it less right than I intend. Ask *me* what you should be doing. I will tell you, and you can be confident in my plans. Save the guilt for that second candy bar from which I clearly told you to walk away.

I have big plans for your wee one. I created your little peanut head in my image to bring glory to my kingdom. Let's not wait to get started. Those extracurriculars can be beneficial to a kid, but those are not the sole purpose of their childhood as I purposed it. Please regroup, and instead of buying that license plate frame that reads

"Taxi-cab Mom," please get one that reads, "I care about what God cares about, and it shows in my kids." Too wordy? Well then, I have always been a fan of "Give peas a chance."

ONE NATION UNDER ME,
GOD

5

Hungry for Some Fruit?

Make a tree good and its fruit will be good,
or make a tree bad and its fruit will be bad,
for a tree is recognized by its fruit.
—MATTHEW 12:33 (NIV)

*W*hat is your fruit? Or should I ask, What behaviors do you see in your children as a by-product of the fruit in your own life? When you found out you were expecting, you probably had a whirlwind of ideals flood your mind: morning walks pushing Baby in the stroller, serene bubble baths with your little one playfully splashing, even visions of your soccer-mom-of-the-year award. No doubt—*no doubt*—now that you have had some time with your bundle of joy, your outlook is slightly altered.

You probably didn't have flashes of your future four-year-old daughter mimicking your "whatever" eye roll or your son's public, verbatim retelling of your "Why Mommy Thinks Daddy Is Lazy" speech. Not in a million years could you have predicted how close a resemblance you would share with your daughter when, in her tween years of eight through twelve, she so routinely stands with her hand on one protruding hip, tapping her foot in impatience. I can only imagine what stories are popping into your head from your own special experiences. I'm sure they are humorous now that you have had time to look back on them. Then again, maybe not. There's a power here maybe you don't know about yet.

Definitely not. Too soon for that walk down memory lane. I see that now.

Focus on Your Fruit

Did you know that you are a fruit-producing tree? It's true. As you live your life day to day, word by word, you are producing fruit. Your children's behavior is often a form of that fruit. How they react to good and bad times is a reflection of the fruit we have planted in their lives and in our own. There's no separating this. We can't continue parenting as if our actions mean nothing and hope our kids will skip over our less-than-righteous characteristics.

> Throughout the years I have grown in many ways because of the Christian environments I was in. Without those, I believe things would be very different indeed. —Noah, 24, Missionary kid

I know this because I have had a certain conversation multiple times with my sweet-faced three-year-old daughter. Her hair is all askew with wild-thing curls, and her cheeks are just freckled enough to make her nose crinkle look like it's been Photoshopped.

The convo goes a bit like this: "We do not say the word 'stupid.' It's not nice and no one feels good after you call them that."

Afterward, of course, she hears me accidentally say something is stupid, and then I hear her use the word. I lean in because leaning-in parenting is the best sort of parenting. Her cheeks are super chubby, and her enormous blue eyes whisper in her toddler way, "Come at me, Mama." So I have to. Almost nose-to-nose and almost at a snail's pace, I quietly say, "Miss Layla Grace. We. Do. Not. Say that word."

Because she is a compliant child, she doesn't say it again. Rather, still nose-to-nose, she mouths it slowly, just slowly enough to show me I have met my match. And that *I* did this.

I created this little turkey out of the overflow of my words and actions. She is a perfect representation of the fruit I am producing, even if that makes me _____ (I will allow you to fill in the blank).

Some options: offended, angry, furious, prideful, never want to go in public again, other.

I can't lie. It was a feat to keep from cracking up in her face, and I was a little proud of her because in that minute I thought, "Man, she is controlling. I'm thinking this means she won't ever do drugs."

Fruit of a Missionary Mom

In Matthew 7, Jesus lays out a line of how-tos in the form of parables. These are stories that deliver messages of *what is* and of *what should be instead*. Some give direction, some appeal for a heart change, but all of them call for a response as God's Word sinks into our hearts to change us.

The particular parable I have in mind is often called "The Tree and Its Fruit." Its point, says Jesus, is this: "A good tree produces good fruit, and a bad tree produces bad fruit" (Matt. 7:17). I am not exactly producing good fruit in those moments of pride or anger. I am human. We are all human, and we all make mistakes. But the high points can outweigh the low points in our parenting if we'll carefully take stock of both what is outgoing and what is incoming.

We get to decide what *kind* of fruit we produce. Did you know that? It's simple because the options are few—healthy or unhealthy. We get to choose to follow after Christ and love the way he does, or we choose the other way. We risk becoming the ones who damage our kids. Matthew continues on to say, "Thus, by their fruit you will recognize them" (Matt. 7:20 NIV). I want Jesus to recognize me by my fruit. I want to look at my chubby-cheeked little girl and see that she is thriving in her walk with Jesus because of the example I have laid out before her.

Take Stock

Take an inventory: What sort of fruit are you producing? Do you yell or belittle, causing bruises? Or do you speak encouraging words to promote growth? Do you water your fruit with hugs and kisses for no reason at all, taking extra care to sprinkle it with I-love-yous? Or are you too preoccupied between phone calls and the call of the internet to nurture your fruit, hoping it will somehow take care of itself? That is mom behavior, not Missionary Mom behavior.

In the beginning, it may be helpful to pick one day and be purposeful with your speaking. Decide that you are going to encourage your children and spend the whole day smothering your kids with genuine compliments. Take a cue from the classic line in the movie *Bambi*. Thumper's mother was brilliant when she asked Thumper to quote his dad's saying, "If you can't say something nice, don't say nothin' at all."

If you aren't sure whether you fall in this category, take a day and listen to how your kids talk to each other and to your husband. Of course, kids will be kids, but this should give you a general idea. And remember, you can't overencourage your kids, provided the encouragement is genuine.

This may be the ultimate test. ::awkward side glance::

Give What Needs Giving

I met with a mama today who is so whelmed that *over*whelmed doesn't even begin to touch her situation. I teach her little boy, and she stays home with her other children. She has two mostly grown children, and Dad is not in the picture. Did your shoulders just droop a little out of solidarity? Mine do every time she and I meet about her struggling boy.

We teachers try to do that thing where we tell you something good about your kiddo before we break the hard stuff to you as gently as possible. Then we swoop in with another positive comment. It's not a formula; it's genuine in most instances. But we know how vulnerable it is for you to hand your babies over to us for the bulk of the daylight hours. We want to honor your work; we want you to remember your son's or daughter's strength before we get to why we are here. So today I did this.

She speaks only Spanish and I speak only English, so we sat with an interpreter finishing off our perfect equilateral triangle, and I prayed nothing would get lost in translation. It went a little something like this (her portions translated, as I also do not write Spanish).

Me: "Hi, Mama. Thank you for coming in to meet with us. I am so grateful for what Will adds to my class. He is so sweet; he draws me a new picture every day. He has crazy art talent. His artwork covers the walls behind my desk."

She manages a meek "Thank you," and I can tell she is already dreading what is to come. She's seen the note home, and she's spoken to the principal. We talk about what seems to be the point of our meeting: Will stole something out of my desk. He confessed easily, but he stole. Will is also failing fifth grade because he isn't turning in his work. She's frustrated with her son and feels her hands are somewhat tied.

I don't mean to sideswipe her, but I ask the interpreter to translate one last point. "I notice Will seems to really thrive when I spend quality time with him and fill him up ahead of time with what I expect for his work time, and then when I check in with him to give a quick word of encouragement. Will has said something to me several times that is important for you to know. He has expressed that he is sad and feels somewhat invisible. He feels a little forgotten, and he actually told me that if no one cares if he does well in school, then he doesn't either."

This is the part where everyone in the office cries. She doesn't mean for any of this to happen, but she can't figure out how to make it stop. And Will isn't trying to make his mama sad. He's trying to get her to notice him—to remember that he needs to be filled up. He is so hungry for her affections, and she's killing herself trying to meet his needs in ways that aren't even important to him: iPad, freedom to do anything he wants at home, his own room, a scooter to play with outside.

Those aren't the things that fill him up. He needs face time. That's it. Trips to the grocery store, Sunday drives, a walk around the marina, a Starbucks run, a date to the movies. None of it has to be big, but when she starts taking this kind of interest in him, he will turn around and pour himself into his responsibilities, aka school.

We cannot afford to casually exist next to our children. We need to take action. The right kind of action. We need to see our kids for who they are and meet them in their spaces.

Pray for God to open your eyes to the accomplishments your children make throughout the day. Be specific with your words, so as your kids grow, they will have no doubt about your feelings toward them. They will be able to trust your words because you have been *for* them this whole time!

Yes. Date your kids. From super early ages, not just to spend one-on-one time with them but to teach them what dating looks like: hold the door, pay, who decides where we are going? Is it OK to eat your date's leftovers without permission? (Uh, no.)

Love, joy, peace, patience, kindness, goodness, faithfulness, gentleness, and self-control (Gal. 5:22–23).

Are you proud of them? Are you happy to see them cooperating? Have you noticed them showing love, patience, kindness, self-control, or any of the other fruits of the spirit Paul talks about in Galatians? Tell them! Then sit back and watch them respond.

How We See Love

Our kids (and all humans) receive love differently. Many books exist that teach this concept so well. My favorite is Gary Chapman's *The Five Love Languages*. He has a version out there specific to kids, but each version has the same basic info. We are each created to best receive love in one of five different ways. The following chart gives a quick glimpse at those five ways.

Love Language	Evidence
Acts of Service	You feel loved when someone does things to help you.
Physical Touch	Holding hands, hugs, affectionate pats, and other physical contact make you feel loved. In marriage, this can include sexual intimacy, but both sexual and nonsexual types of affection are important to a spouse that loves this way.
Quality Time	Totally undivided attention makes you feel cared about. Face time, walks, dates: these fill you up.
Gifts	Any gift and all gifts, regardless of monetary value, make you feel as though someone took the time to think of you, and that means they love you.
Words of Affirmation	Encouraging words, I love yous, thank yous, and specific compliments make you feel loved.

A few notes to consider. Adults tend to have one, maybe two, love languages. Children may seem to be all five for a while depending on their age. As they get older one tends to win out. It's usually impossible to tell a child's love language before the age of three or four. Just assume they need all of it. And at no point is a person exempt from the other four languages. Who doesn't love a hug or kiss or a note of encouragement?

Our children are heavily affected by our words and body language. When my eyebrows have scowled for so long that my forehead is permanently corrugated, and my words are short with underlying anger, my kids will either obey out of fear or tune me out altogether. Neither of these responses is attractive or equips children to be functioning adults. But if I choose a pleasant countenance followed by words of encouragement, my children will likely continue to demonstrate this behavior. I see them become hungry for my praise.

On more than one occasion, my son has tried to one-up his sister while she is suffering a punishment. I'll reprimand her for laziness with her chores, and he will jump up and very obviously begin to do extra chores. Certainly, part of his motivation stems from wanting to outshine his sister. But even more, he is fishing for compliments. He is seizing his opportunity because he is a words-of-affirmation kid to the core.

I don't want my children to feel they have to beg for my recognition; I want to give it willingly as just another way to build them up and show them how much I love them.

A word of warning: please be genuine. Our words of praise can become unwanted if we aren't genuine. Kids know. Like sharks can smell blood a long way off, children can sense if we aren't genuine in our compliments from a mile away. Saying something just to fit a word in before the day is up, or being vague, can turn our best intentions into a wedge between hearts. And if our kids don't trust our encouragement, they'll begin to mistrust us on other fronts as well.

Kid Fruit

It's never too soon for our kids to start producing their own fruit. They have the ability from the early preschool years to build up their friends, teachers, siblings, and you. Most of us have stories of our young one saying something so timely that it just melted our busy hearts. We have the opportunity from the get-go to build this into their makeup as a norm, not a random occurrence.

Going back to those love languages, there's a good chance your kiddo will attempt to love others in the way he or she receives love. Start there. Do they tend to give a compliment on someone's outfit or new glasses? Pull them aside and tell them you are proud of them for noticing. Explain what it must feel like to whoever heard those sweet words. Such words have the opportunity to change someone's day, week, maybe even stick with them forever. Romans 12:8 says, "If your gift is to encourage others, be encouraging." How simply stated is that?

6

Power in Prayer

Pray in the Spirit at all times and on every occasion.
Stay alert and be persistent in your prayers
for all believers everywhere.
—EPHESIANS 6:18

*W*ant a sure return on an investment? Invest your time in prayer for your family. Don't waste your time being vague with these petitions to God. Instead keep in mind three aspects: past, present, and future. Or in our case, future, present, and past. Settle in and get after it.

Future

This entire book is centered on the idea that your child will grow up to be our future. Feeling a little bit of pressure? The fact remains: our children will be the leaders one day. Teachers, politicians, *the* president, principals, military leaders, pastors, Sunday school teachers, Meals on Wheels coordinators, and parents are just a few of the powerful roles our children will hold once they hit adulthood. They will be our care-givers. They will be the decision makers.

One day, our kids will no longer have us around to answer their questions. They will have to pray through and make the decisions that are best for their family or their work or their children or their parents.

Before you throw this book across the room in denial, let me just say, our parents were probably just as terrified when they came to this realization. We are not *totally* screwing it up, are we? This is our reality, so let's weigh our options.

We can ignore the inevitable, cross our fingers, and hope our kids pick up on what we *say* is the best way to live. Or, we can be intentional in our parenting and pray for our children's futures very specifically. There are hundreds of ways to pray for our kids. Let's take a closer look at a few.

When We Focus Our Prayers

The spiritual gifts your child receives from God will be used to either affect multitudes or be placed on a metaphorical shelf. The very existence of this shelf is devastating. It's the devil's shelf; do whatever you can to get rid of it. Pray that your child discovers his gifts early—maybe even with your help. There's no rule about what age you have to be to know God's call on your life. There is certainly no age God prefers. If anything, Jesus showed us the worth of children above all others. The littlest kids seem to pick up on this.

Four-year-olds are pretty much awesome. Picture a boy at this age. He cannot tie his own shoes, and it wouldn't matter because they are always on the wrong feet. Pants are an option, and he thinks it's funny to put vegetables in his nose and blow them out. This kid is my eldest son. When he was four, he began introducing himself to our smallish church of three hundred.

The only thing funnier is doing this on repeat.

Picture it. It's Sunday morning, and the hustle slows as the volunteers settle into place. My son is always at the sanctuary doors. "Hi," he says, shaking hands with a grown man he does not know. "My name is Elijah. I am a pastor here."

Even when I'm across the room, I know this is what he says because their jaws drop. Just a little. Like they're being punk'd. But they aren't. They are just seeing my real life.

He stands ready at the door just in front of the greeter team, usurping their territory. They assume he is waiting for his mom or has some reason for being there. And he does. Clearly he needs people to know he is a pastor here.

What? No, you cannot make this stuff up. Of course, once people associate the two of us, I hear all about it.

"So, a little boy came up to me today. I was told he is your son." I confirm it as a gray-haired gentleman smiles and points out my little Elijah across the room.

"Yes, that is my little boy. Was he being naughty? Was he rude? Just say it," I mumble, nervous, not because my son is a troublemaker, but I'm grasping at why this man I've never met is so eager to share his conversation with me.

"No, no," the gentleman says. "He was actually quite kind. He shook my hand and let me know he is a pastor at this church," the man adds with a chuckle. "He spoke quite assuredly."

"Oh, goodness." How else can I respond? I wish I could say I'm confident, but my eyes are darting here and there, pits sweating, laughter awkward. "Well, he is quite a character. Thank you for telling me. Is this your first time here?"

"No. Actually, I used to be the pastor at this church before they switched me to district leader over this area. My son *is* actually the pastor here."

This is where I realize that, because I am the children's pastor here, this man—his name is Dave—is actually my boss's boss. I had no idea. I bury my face in my hands and only remove them when I hear my son in the distance, once again welcoming new members into his congregation. Awesome.

That was Elijah at four, and the best part of the above scenario was, he never smirked after introducing himself, no matter how much his newfound friend laughed at the thought of a four-year-old saying such a thing. Instead, Elijah took it a step further:

Eli (face serious, demeanor casual): Dave, I am going to be your boss one day. When I grow up, I am going to be your boss.

Dave (face hardly surprised, demeanor casual): Really? You aren't going to just come and work here; you are actually going to take over and be my boss?

Eli: Yep. The boss.

Dave: Good to know.

Dave looked up at my husband and me and said something like, "I pretty much believe him." I laughed for half an hour and then went to Target and bought Eli a T-shirt that read, "Someday I will be your boss."

For real, that shirt was on sale that day. Clearly the T-shirt was from Jesus. Clearly I had *nothing* to do with this idea of my son introducing himself as "a pastor here." Clearly something was stirring in his little four-year-old mind to make him confident of his calling in life. I was beginning to see that God intended to use me, Eli's mother, to train him up according to God's ways so Elijah would have the best possible chance to *always* walk in the will of God.

I never want to take my job lightly. I pray daily for my son to know—with more faith than Moses standing in front of that sea of deadly waters before him and with murderous warriors behind him—where God has called him. I pray for my son to stand like David in front of any giant that satan has planned, armed with a fistful of rocks, a sling, and the power of *the* Almighty God in every fiber

You word nerds may want to send me an email to say I should have capitalized satan because it's his name. As the vice president of Word Nerds Anonymous, I would like to confess that leaving his name lowercase is my small rebellion against him because I do not feel he deserves a capital letter. Like the acronym LOL, I am sure this will catch on.

of his being. I pray this way because I believe God has a plan for my Elijah. I can't prove it, but I feel an urgency to support the work God has begun in my son.

Now fast forward Eli's life seven years. Our family has moved states and switched churches, and we know only a handful of people. After six Sundays (not in a row) of attending our new church, a man whom I would guess to be in his sixties approaches me. One sentence into our conversation, my sweaty armpits are back, and I can't help feeling like I am being set up.

Gentleman (face serious, demeanor casual): Are you Elijah's mom?

Me (so hesitantly): Yes?

Gentleman: Oh, he is something else. I just wanted to tell you that he is an incredible kid.

I don't mean this to come across as a question, but I am sort of wanting to know where this conversation is going first.

Me (relieved, then beaming): *Yes!* Thank you so much for telling me that. I kind of like him.

Gentleman (moving in closer to prove his intensity. It is very intense, considering we have not officially met. Obviously. I am calling him "Gentleman" instead of his name—because I still don't know it!): I mean it. Do you already know that he is special? God has set him apart.

Me (narrowing eyes, trying to match his intensity): I do, actually. When he was four, he began introducing himself as the pastor at our last church. I don't think he knew he was being funny.

Gentleman (gasping in complete surprise, or perhaps understanding; I'm not sure which): I *believe* it! I mean it; you need to protect that boy. God has big plans for him. He is such a polite boy. He looked in my eyes when he shook my hand, and I told him I needed to talk to you. I made him point you out so I could tell you what a special kid he is.

Me: I absolutely believe it; and thank you so much for letting me know. It means a lot.

Gentleman: Well, you are very welcome.

God has taken the time to have strangers approach me about the possible futures of my children. I know I'm not alone in this parenting phenomenon. I don't know if Elijah will become a pastor, but it doesn't matter. My response is to pray diligently for my children, their walk with God, their wisdom in the Word, and the impact they will have on every person around them.

None of these stories is meant to brag. Instead, I mean to show the amount of support God offers moms. He invites us in to be part of his plan for our children. As an encouragement, God brings perfect strangers to point us in the right direction. His direction. What an amazing blessing!

I am reminded regularly to pray for my kids and for the women and men they will become. Because God has chosen them. And God has chosen *your* children. You shouldn't feel like you need random strangers to stop you before you pray fervently for your kids. Let this be your invitation. Please. Allow me to be your random stranger. Pray for your children's future.

Present

Prayers for the present are fickle because the present quickly becomes the past. My repeated prayer for my kids' present is focused more on my recognizing teachable moments and my children responding in a teachable way. Otherwise, I spend my "present" prayers focused on teaching my children to pray.

Did you know we need to teach our children to pray? Of course we do. Jesus taught his disciples to pray in the book of Luke. He gave one example of prayer beginning with, "Father, hallowed be your name" (11:2 NIV). Many are familiar with this prayer. We learn to pray watching Jesus teach the disciples how to pray. In the same way, our kids listen to us pray and mimic what they hear. This will not happen if we do not pray aloud with our children. Prayer should be a regular part of every day in your household. The most obvious place to introduce prayer is before meals and before bed.

With seven people in our house, we assigned a prayer night to each person throughout the week. Every Friday night my five-year-old prays. I mention him because his prayers are hilarious and usually about food or something he has asked us for and received a "no" answer.

One Friday night, we gathered in the living room as usual to pray. It's quiet for a few seconds, and just as I am about to look to see what's holding us up, Sam pipes in, "Dear Jesus, thank you for our day. Please help me get extra dessert even though my mom said I am grounded from sugar for having no self-control. Let us have a good night sleep. Help Eli be nicer to me. Help Squirrel close her eyes when we are praying right now because I am looking, and they are open. Almonds. I mean amen." *Sigh.*

We are still working on him, but the point is that he is praying. He knows how to pray (mostly), he knows where to go when he needs someone to talk to, and he isn't going to have to call a church leader because he thinks the pastor is the only one to whom God listens.

In addition to bedtime and mealtimes, we take time to pray throughout the day as my husband and I feel led. If I get a text from a friend saying she is struggling, we stop to say a quick prayer. If I get a phone call saying someone has a job interview, we stop and give thanks. If my husband tells of a fire raging on a mountain somewhere, we stop to pray for the firefighters, fire captains, and the people who live around the fire. Sometimes we even pray for rain. And speaking of firefighters, we pray for my husband.

"I See a Fire Truck!"

My husband became a firefighter almost ten years ago, and since then, many people ask if I worry about him having such a dangerous job. I can honestly say the thought has never occurred to me because I know God has saved my husband's life at least three times in the past forty years. He is totally capable of writing my husband's story and caring for my heart while he is at it. Remember? *He* knows the plans.

God will protect my husband according to his will, just as he will protect my children according to the plan he has for each of them. Worry gets me nowhere. I lean on God, and I pray for favor. I also teach my children to pray for my husband by using a visual.

Every time we see a fire truck, we each take a turn saying a quick prayer for Our Firefighter. New riders in our SUV are often frightened when one of us hollers, "I see a fire truck!" Full volume. I can only guess they are certain death is imminent. Their fear increases as each of us hollers, "I see a fire truck second . . . third . . ." and so on.

Then we pray for Our Firefighter in that order. If we happen to be praying for Our Firefighter and another truck drives by, we shout again and pray twice. We even do it when Our Firefighter is in the car with us. There is a slight chance he thinks we are crazy, but who does not enjoy someone (or six someones) praying for him?

You can do the same sort of association with the people in your family. My dad calls every time he hears the song "Butterfly Kisses." Since the year that song came out on the radio, he has called just to remind me he loves me. Now that we have a daughter named Layla Grace, he calls my kids to say hello every time he hears Eric Clapton start to sing about a certain little temptress.

I would like to take this minute to publicly apologize to the innocent passenger. I am sorry your coffee spit out of your mouth that one time we wanted to pray for Our Firefighter. Thank you for helping to clean the windshield. I'm glad you stopped choking.

Sometimes it is difficult to think of praying for children and grandchildren you do not even have yet. But if you, like my dad, choose something that sparks a reminder for you every time you hear it or see it, you can do what we do and shoot out a quick prayer for those future kiddos. It helps to choose something you see often, like a certain flower, the American flag, a park, or a type of business such as a preschool.

Then every time you pass a park, say a quick prayer. "Lord, thank you for being great enough to handle any schemes against my babies and grandbabies yet to come. Use me to leave a legacy of loving you and loving others. You are the protector and greatest influence over my children and grandchildren. I praise you for who they will become. Amen."

> **I think God has given me the desire to be a great mom. My heart is to be the best mom I can be with God's guidance.**
> **—Mindy, Missionary Mom of three**

If you are in the car with the kids, pray aloud. Tell them what you are doing. Encourage them to choose reminders to pray for others. Pray for their friends. Pray for their teachers. Pray for their siblings. Pray for orphans who have no mama but need someone to cover them just as you do for your own children. This prayer pattern is the perfect example of ceaseless prayer. Teach your kids to pray, and maybe they will start praying for you too!

Past

Because I take a closer look at our biblical past in other chapters, I will speak only briefly here on how prayer and heritage work together. Learning from the mistakes and successes of biblical characters gives children experiences and know-how when tough situations arise.

Laying hold of biblical history is vital to children's grasping onto the future God has planned for them since they were a twinkle in your eye. These stories are our heritage; these people, our ancestors. As we read the pages of God's Word, we lay claim to the idea that this is our own personal history. Then we can turn around and pass along this biblical heritage to our children. Our kids don't need to start from square one. God has graciously passed down stories of right (and wrong) living.

One such Old Testament standout is Joseph. His move to get the heck out of Dodge when Potiphar's wife began making passes at him is an excellent example for teens who find themselves in over their heads in intimate situations.

And let's not forget Jacob and Esau. Their battle for inheritance is a how-not-to-be-a-good-brother tutorial that portrays the long-term repercussions of a young man's poor choice to lie—and, soberingly, of his mother's involvement in the deceit.

Pray for your children to know such biblical stories as their personal history. Pray that your children will pull wisdom from those stories when they face similar situations.

Before-Bed Scriptures

One tool we can use in our prayer time is Scripture. Each night, or week, or whatever time frame works best for you, choose one Scripture to pray over your kids. Choose the same one for each of your children, or try choosing one per kid. Choose one for your nephews and nieces. Choose one for the kids in your neighborhood. Then pray these Scriptures before you go to bed each night. Whether you pray them together with your kids or simply between you and Jesus, this is a power move. Hide these words in your heart on behalf of the kids God has placed in your life. Put their names in the verses and own those verses on the children's behalf.

On the next page is a list of verses you can pull from:

Deuteronomy 4:35–36
Deuteronomy 8:7–8
Joshua 1:9
2 Chronicles 20:12
Nehemiah 4:14
Psalm 1:1–2
Psalm 4:5
Psalm 5:12
Psalm 7:10
Psalm 19:14
Psalm 23
Psalm 27:14
Psalm 119:57
Proverbs 1:33
Isaiah 8:17
Isaiah 12:2
Isaiah 54:17
Jeremiah 29:11–14
Hosea 6:3
Matthew 11:28–29
John 14:27

Acts 2:38–39
Acts 15:11
Romans 8:28
2 Corinthians 9:6
Ephesians 6:10–13
Philippians 1:6
Colossians 1:16
Colossians 3:2
Colossians 3:12
2 Thessalonians 1:6
2 Thessalonians 3:16
1 Timothy 6:11
2 Timothy 3:16
2 Timothy 4:18
Hebrews 10:36
Hebrews 11:1
James 3:18
James 4:10
2 Peter 3:8–9
1 John 4:4
Revelation 4:11

7

Lead by Example

Lead me in the right path, O LORD, or my enemies will
conquer me. Make your way plain for me to follow.
—PSALM 5:8

$\mathcal{P}$**ur·pose** ['pur-puhs], *n.*—practical results, effect, or advantage. This word has the potential to cause sleepless nights. We get caught up in the thoughts of minutes flying by, leaving no time to do all the extras or even the essentials. We wake with saucers for eyes after a nightmare that starts with Junior's graduation and ends with him walking down a mysterious path. He's looking over his shoulder with wild eyes as if to say, "I wish you would have sent me to fewer Chuck E. Cheese birthday parties and told me a little more about how to recognize God's path for my life. That knowledge would have been super helpful about now."

Don't fret. And please don't feel condemned if you just attended two birthday parties in your three hours of downtime this weekend. Instead, open your perspective to think more globally and much more long term. Like an ER doctor who has just been assigned a patient who appears fatal, think vitals.

Fundamental Focus

Ever feel like you need a vacation from your vacation or a week off after your weekend? Maybe it is time to check your vitals.

I don't mean your heart rate or blood sugar (although some of our health issues could be resolved with a few simple life changes to weed out stress). The vitals I am referring to include teaching your child to love, lead, and be the change people are always squawking about.

But we cannot pass along what we are not living. What is vital to life? What will lead to a truly full life, and what will leave you—and your child—wanting?

Cover to cover, the Bible is filled with men, women, and even kids who lived audacious, godly lives. Learn their stories. I'd begin with David. What are *his* best characteristics? How does he live out his early years so he is prepared for the later years—the really hard ones? We have to experience this so we can teach it to our kids.

Picture yourself in your proudest parenting moment, and teach your kids about those victories. Let go of the world and cling to the words God wants you to hear and obey. Be willing to make a complete life halt to make space for what matters most—discipleship.

We may need to grasp the message that we're so busy being Christian mothers we aren't taking time to be Christlike mamas. Setting an example of loving the unlovable. Giving more than what is comfortable. Sacrificing for God's glory, not ours, and creating a proverbial calendar for the next eighteen years that fully devotes us to being the best mothers we can possibly be.

Why the Devil Will Not Like This

The devil doesn't want this to work out. He does not want you to take time with your kids, to equip your kids, to "start children off on the way they should go" (Prov. 22:6 NIV). Every promise the Bible offers flies in the face of the enemy. He has plans to steal your time and energy by subtly convincing you to spend time in worry, time in anger, time with nonsense, time in distraction. He plans to kill. And by kill, I mean murder. John 10:10 says, "The thief comes only to steal and kill and destroy" (NIV). Well, he sounds fun.

That evil little schlep has as many plans for our lives as we do, maybe as many as God has for us. He has great (evil, but great) plans for our children. We know this because we hear these verses, and we hear our pastor teach on it. We know this because we see sin appear at surprisingly young ages in our little children. What scares me is how quickly we lose sight of the fact that we are in this war.

We are in a war.

We must fight for our children.

That rotten little liar, satan, confounds our thinking as parents just enough to make us feel we are doing the right thing as long as we are not doing the overtly wrong thing.

We raise our kids to be good people; what is wrong with that? Nothing. But are we raising them to stand firm on the Word of the Lord? Do they have protective measures in place to fight back when the devil puts potentially devastating thoughts into their minds? Are they confident in the fact that they are loved? Do they know they each have a guardian angel who speaks to God every day on their behalf (Matt. 18:10)? What an encouraging thing to know!

Less encouraging is the knowledge that our children are in the war just as much as we are. Interesting news on that: "We are not fighting against flesh-and-blood enemies, but against evil rulers and authorities of the unseen world, against mighty powers in this dark world, and against evil spirits in the heavenly places" (Eph. 6:12).

In a way, sometimes hearing from God feels like a game of chess. Jesus is the king and I want most to follow where he leads. God speaks out his direction: "Knight to e5!" I hear it, and sometimes I obey, or start to obey, but then the devil shouts above all the noise, and I find myself heading the wrong direction or looking the wrong way. Then I spend the next week in frustration and disappointment with my choices, and I just stare longingly at the place God *intended* me to land.

Bah! Stinking distractions. Stinking, big-mouthed devil. And it isn't even his fault! He is being exactly who I know him to be. The enemy's plans are not complex. All he did was scream a little louder than God spoke, and I fell for it. I fall for it often.

I am caught up in his game of simple distraction before I realize I am moving away from God's still small voice. ("After the fire came a gentle whisper" [1 Kings 19:12 NIV].) What's more, I often waste time kicking myself over what I should have chosen even after I have stopped listening to the devil's ideas. Because the devil isn't anything if he isn't a man with a plan.

More on loudmouth people in the discipline chapter.

> Me: What was I thinking? I heard God; I was ready. I was moving.
> satan: Idiot. Like fish in a barrel.

Add copious amounts of shame and agony which, really, keep me just as far from getting back to God.

And he is *totally* right! It makes me want to yell from a mountaintop. I want to be Kevin in *Home Alone* when he faces the imaginary furnace monster in the basement, yelling, "I'm not afraid anymore! Did you hear me?"

The devil isn't going to change. Ever. He just isn't. I need to get to the point where I am not afraid anymore and scream it at the top of my lungs: "You don't win, sir! You will never win. I am choosing to focus on Jesus."

Here is the silly realization. The rules of chess say it's game over when the king has fallen, right? Well the King—Jesus—*has* been slain. But in a true plot twist, rather than this meaning defeat for us, it signals the start to my freedom and the devil's destruction.

The King has been slain, and what's more, in the real world, our King rose again.

This bears repeating: *He rose again.*

That is the power we have on *our* side.

Nevertheless, here I sit, allowing the loser in this war to lead me around by the nose while I stare longingly at what could have been. Please tell me I am not the only one this happens to. *Please.*

The devil has plans for me. He doesn't sleep. He plots *Humor me.* for my life. Consider that I am an adult, I know Scripture, and I have the wherewithal to fight him and deny him and choose God.

Now, consider your children. Take a minute and picture each of them facing any number of the struggles you have faced in your life.

Certainly, the enemy is plotting against your children. Do they innately have what it takes to fight him and deny him and choose God? No, but you have what it takes to raise them so they learn it. I promise. God promises. He says, "Never will I leave you; never will I forsake you" (Heb. 13:5 NIV). He says, "It is God who works in you to will and to act in order to fulfill his good purpose" (Phil. 2:13 NIV). He says he is gentle and humble and that his burden is light—much more suited for carrying than our own (Matt. 11:30). He tells us he cares more for the one sheep that wandered away than the ninety-nine that did not wander off. He is specifically referring to our children when he says, "In the same way your Father in heaven is not willing that any of these little ones should perish" (Matt. 18:14 NIV).

We need to teach our children the strategies of this war and help them to recognize the enemy's tactics for what they are: obnoxiously loud, meaningless moves by the loser after the game is over. We need to lead by example. Our children are watching our every move, and they are copying each of them.

World Changers

While doing a little research on women who accomplished much and changed the world in some way, I read this story in Gilda Radner's *It's Always Something*:

OK, I really read this because she had really big hair like me, and when I was small my mom called me Roseanne Roseannadanna. And no kidding. I have a picture of us looking like identical hair twins.

When I was little, Dibby's cousin had a dog, just a mutt, and the dog was pregnant. I don't know how long dogs are pregnant, but she was due to have her puppies in about a week. She was out in the yard one day and got in the way of the lawn mower and her two hind legs got cut off. They rushed her to the vet and he said, "I can sew her up, or you can put her to sleep if you want, but the puppies are okay. She'll be able to deliver the puppies."

Dibby's cousin said, "Keep her alive."

So the vet sewed up her backside, and over the next week the dog learned to walk. She didn't spend any time worrying, she just learned to walk by taking two steps in the front and flipping up her backside, and then taking two steps and flipping up her backside again. She gave birth to six little puppies, all in perfect health. She nursed them and then weaned them. And when they learned to walk, they all walked like her.[4]

Whatever example we set will be what our kids mimic: our laugh, our sneeze, our walk, our words. From birth, we are learning from the adults around us; that is human nature. If those leading are too far-fetched or cause too much pain, we may look elsewhere.

> My mom has taught me to serve and treat others before myself. She constantly prompts us to give—time, gifts, food, kindness, advice—whenever someone is in need.
> —Layla, 15, Missionary kid

Unfortunately, especially when we are hurting, our judgment is not brilliant. Our kids aren't exempt from this and often turn to peers, who may not have the best advice. Typically, though, in healthy situations, parents hold the greatest influence. A puppy learns how to walk from his mama. A child learns how to *everything* from his mother. So the next time your bundle of joy throws a tantrum and you want to chalk it up to human nature, you may want to remind yourself that you are the human whom Baby is naturally following.

All of this can begin to feel a little heavy, but we can shift our focus just a bit when we become overwhelmed. Think purpose, not pressure. Think opportunity, not defeat.

You may feel your children are pulled in every direction except the right one, and you may think your input is small. Not true. Be reassured, God has placed that little bundle in *your* hands. Not the hands of the lady next door who seems to have it all together. Not the hands of the pastor whose prayers get heard before yours because he is a man of the cloth.

For real, that lady probably has the same issues you do.

Children will mimic your habits, your food choices, your handwriting, your love for your favorite football team, and your stance on organic produce. If you live life on purpose, they will also mimic what really matters:

By the way, we all "wear cloth." Each of us has a direct path to God in heaven, so we no longer need a middle man.

> your faith
> your peace
> your mercy
> your grace

> your willingness
> your love
> your joy
> your kindness

> your patience
> your goodness
> your gentleness
> and your self-control

How do I know? Because the Bible tells me so. Proverbs 20:7 says, "The godly walk with integrity; blessed are their children who follow them."

(Seemingly) Small Gestures Welcomed

What can you do today to be purposeful in your child's life? Sure, you could pack your bags and whisk little Jimmy away on the next plane to be a missionary. But, wouldn't holding the door for the lady with the stroller teach him to be considerate of others and pass along kindness? Wouldn't tithing at your church teach him to have a giving heart and trust in God for provision?

Wouldn't stopping your day to pray for someone in need, and then giving whatever you could to help that person, create the same testimony as those of overseas missionaries? What if you simply set out to help the people right in front of you who have a need today? If missionaries travel far and wide to show people the love of Jesus, couldn't you just look around and show nearby people the love of Jesus? Who knows—maybe the next time you walk through a door it will be little Jimmy who says, "Here, let me get that for you. My mom taught me this."

Discipline . . . on Purpose

No discipline seems pleasant at the time, but painful. Later on, however, it produces a harvest of righteousness and peace for those who have been trained by it.
—HEBREWS 12:11 (NIV)

*D*iscipline means something different to just about everyone, and the connotation of the word changes more still depending on the specific circumstance and a person's background. As a verb, according to Dictionary.com, discipline means "to train by instruction and exercise; drill."

Apply this to parenting and you can see the intention of God's purposes in our disciplining our children. We are to set an example, give clear guidance, mark boundaries, and revisit every lesson through drill and exercise. I'm not saying we should create scenarios for our kids to struggle. Those situations come naturally, and we can make the most of them when they arise. Instead, our focus should be divvied up (and not evenly) between *proactive* and *retroactive* discipline.

Proactive Discipline

Several of our previous chapters showcase forms of proactive discipline, featuring Scriptures at the ready and parents leading by example. The idea is for these approaches to become habits that give a child a solid foundation to stand upon. No sandy shores here, sucker (Matt. 7:24–27). Instead our kids have what Jesus called wisdom: they build a house on a rock rather than on shifting sands that erode with the weather and waves. Being a prepared and preemptive parent means doing much of the work up front, so there is less cleanup after the fact. We begin the process of discipline and discipleship way back when we still count our kids' ages in months, so that their tween and teen years are way more tolerable.

Sorry about the name-calling. I am passionate about sandy shores.

We know little Johnny is going to make mistakes. If we have any connection with the world around us, we can agree that little Lucy will need to be disciplined, and probably soon. This is natural. Maybe the real problem is our preconceived ideas as parents.

Why don't we count our ages in months anymore? I am 488 months old. I'll give you a moment to calculate yours.

Let Your Talking Do the Talking

Often children's mistakes are exacerbated because, as parents, we have expectations that we don't always convey to them. But boy do we presume our kids will live up to those expectations! Wouldn't childhood be so much easier if our kids knew what was clearly expected of them at nearly every turn? This is not the same as being a controlling parent. What I am proposing is clear communication ahead of the game.

Let's use a sports analogy. I understand baseball, so let's head out to the field. All of the players are my children. God is the umpire and I am the coach. As the coach of this summertime game, I see the importance of starting training early in the spring.

I have expectations: I want team players, zero injuries, and at least a few wins. I want to have fun, laugh more than we cry, and see my team grow. Those goals are clear, set ahead of the season, and there is no way

I am waiting until top of the ninth, game one, to share these hopes. I would be fired, right?

Parenting should run parallel to this baseball season. Your dream season won't just show up; first you have to put some action behind what you are imagining.

Tell them.

When you picture your kid in social settings, how does he act? When you visualize being a mother, what are you doing? Maybe it is time to forego the false impressions we have about parenting and get to the nitty-gritty. Spring training starts as soon as your baby opens her eyes. Thinking it may be a bit past that time? No worries. Start when your baby wakes up tomorrow morning or the next time you see her.

Let's Do This: Retroactive Discipline

My youngest son, Samuel, has a smidgeon of a temper. His crazier, rabid side seems to come out when his siblings have ignored him one time too many, and, considering he is the youngest of the troop, I do not fault him fully. It is difficult to get a word in around here unless you are willing to speak up. To Samuel, this means saying your sentence eleven times, screaming the offender's name in an irritated, squeaky voice at top volume. Then adding a knuckle sandwich for good measure. Naturally the whole room shuts down, all eyes on Sam. One of my other children usually whispers, "Awkward," with a sarcastic tone. I close my eyes and sigh quietly.

> I feel God has equipped me to be a great mother. He's given me common sense. An amazing spouse. He's given me a reasonable amount of patience and a good upbringing. He's put people around me to advise me and to learn from. He gives me creative ideas to teach and discipline my kids.
> —Melissa, Missionary Mom of two

My next reaction is to focus on the hitting and screaming and defuse the situation by removing the culprit to give him cooldown time. Then, after I have dealt with the injured, it is time to get to the bottom of things. I practice my speech as I head upstairs. *Sam, you psycho! What were you thinking? Sam, we don't hit! Seriously, kid, how many times are we going to reenact this scenario?*

I don't say any of those things when I actually get to him. My little boy is sad and frustrated and probably wishes he had a younger sibling to boss around. He feels rejected and ignored. Still, he has to be accountable.

And I probably know this because he has told me so.

As the adult, it is easy for me to see that all of his actions were really reactions to his siblings' lack of acknowledgment. He feels discarded and disrespected. And this is not the first time. Chances are this is at least the second time in a week we are dealing with this same incident. Our focus is not on his present situation, though. Our focus is on his past.

What happened last time, and what did we decide to do differently this time? The last time he and I talked after a nearly identical situation, Samuel agreed to attempt to get his audience member's attention by saying a name rather than talking blindly to the crowd and hoping to be heard. Last time he agreed that if he was ignored, he would place a hand on their shoulder to get their full attention. He agreed to come to his dad or me and ask for help to be heard. Last time he was put in time-out for however long it took him to defuse and had to apologize to his somewhat clueless victims. This time we are going to focus on making his accountability a little more concrete.

If we want our kids to be able to face an angry situation and still function, we have to put the choices in their hands. A five-minute time-out helps no one if they are still crazy-eyed at the end of it. That means they probably spent their time plotting revenge rather than praying through or chilling out.

When our kids are in trouble, especially because of a repeat offense, they've got to answer some vital questions:

What did you do wrong?
Did that choice affect anyone else?
What could you have done differently?
What do you need to do now that you know this information?
What will you do differently next time?

This is the step Samuel needs to get past the temper he lets loose whenever he feels unnoticed. Because he is young, we work on this together; I read the questions, and he tells me what to write. We head to the dollar store, just the two of us, and buy a picture frame for his report. Then, and possibly most importantly, we hang it in his room and pray. Just the two of us. He gets all of me in this time. Only kindness and only leading in love. No shunning or anger. No passive-aggressive control.

We pray for our patience, for Sam's voice to be heard, for his reactions to others, for his feelings not to be hurt. We pray that our family will communicate and be kind to Sam. We thank God for this awesome kid who battles so hard to be heard, and we pray that he will always keep that fight, but not out of offense. I don't want him to simply hand over his voice. Who knows? Maybe Sam will grow up to be the voice for others, and because he has so much experience at fighting to be heard, he will know how to be loud enough that the world may actually hear him. His voice could help bring about change.

Only God knows. The point is that Samuel is a part of this family, he is created in God's image, and he is on loan to us from God. We are called to make him, not break him.

The Consequence of Building Up

If your idea of parenting is applying so much pressure that your kid snaps under your thumb (or words), you may want to ask God if this is his intention for you. My guess is, you know the answer, but you don't realize this is how you parent. Ask yourself this: "Have I ever bragged to another parent about how harsh I was to my child? Have I ever bragged about how I put someone (anyone) 'in his place'?"

I want to say this kindly (from an it-takes-one-to-know-one perspective): That isn't power. That's pride. And it's definitely not parenting. Pray and ask God to show you if any of it is true of you. You may be acting on habits from your parents and not even realize it.

How often do you find yourself angry and offended when your child misbehaves? And then following up his wrongdoing with an unreasonable punishment? Discipline with purpose, not as a reaction. If your child has a rotten mouth, make him scrub a toilet. Do not ground him for a week. Once the toilet is clean, finish the discipline by talking to your kiddo. Check his work. Talk about dirty toilets being as off-putting as rotten mouths. Get to the bottom of why he is talking the way he is. Maybe he needs more sleep, maybe he needs to get something off his chest, or maybe he needs some sunshine. Then again, maybe he is just having a stubborn day and needs to scrub some more toilets. And once those are clean, if he is still having trouble, then he needs to clean sinks, showers, and bathroom floors.

This type of discipline puts the control with your child. He'll work through it because he has time to process, and he is tired of cleaning toilets. And aren't you thrilled? Your bathroom is a little cleaner.

Isn't the whole point of disciplining to teach our children to course-correct and get back on track with God's plan for their lives? That's why God allows it in our lives. Going off the path hurts, so we feel that pressure and make our way back under God's umbrella. Through love we should discipline our children in the same way.

With All Due Respect

We all fall into the parenting patterns of our own authority figures from our childhood. One minute we are asking our kid, "What just happened?" and the next we are spouting phrases we swore we would never use with our own children:

"Because I am the mom, that's why."

"Because I said so."

"What's wrong with you?"

Incidentally, these are three phrases Missionary Moms should lose from their vocabulary bank.

When I was a kid, Jack Handey, from the show *Saturday Night Live*, used to have a moment in the show when he would share his thoughts. Many were ridiculous, some were political, but sometimes one showed up that deserved a bit of consideration. One that stuck with me is, "A man doesn't automatically get my respect. He has to get down in the dirt and beg for it." Absurd really, but isn't that sometimes how we think as parents? We think, *We shouldn't have to earn the right to be respected!*

We are the PARENTS!

Insert your shock-and-awe face and huffy breath.

Yes, well. Praise God he never subjected us to such piety. He loved us first. He is gracious always. His forgiveness doesn't wear out. And I'm thinking you can attest right along with me that his patience is immeasurable.

I always thought it was interesting how the angels in the Bible reacted to people. After telling their audience (usually an audience of one) not to be afraid, they often follow with, "Get up."

They deserve respect, certainly. They hold a mighty position that warrants reverence, clearly. But they know better than anyone that God is the only one who should be revered above all else. Your kids will respect you because you are their mama, because you are someone worth following, because you loved them first. By all means, correct your daughter when she is disrespectful, but do not come at her with the "put you in your place" stick before she even has the chance to get started.

Make your kid.

Don't break your kid.

Parenting Small

In every scenario ever played out, children broken by their parents require healing. Broken kids should never be a by-product of our parenting. As a parental figure, God guides us. He looks and sees our capabilities, not just our struggles. God convicts. He never condemns. He is quiet. He never gets in our face and screams about his position. He speaks to us through examples of his love. We will be wise to follow suit.

I read a verse reminding me that God sees our good: "Therefore encourage one another and build each other up, just as in fact you are doing" (1 Thess. 5:11 NIV). We are instructed to encourage others and build up, not tear down. God subtly makes the point that encouraging and building others up is entirely possible and pleasing to him.

God didn't send someone to yell at me; he didn't drop an email in my inbox listing all the ways I am discouraging; and he didn't pile on the guilt by jabbing his finger in my face until I rebelled. Instead, he spoke life into me. He built me up. He didn't break me down to show me he is boss; I know he is the boss. Rather, he showed me clearly how to behave through the way he loved me first.

9

Loud Parenting Is Not Discipline

If I speak in the tongues of men or of angels, but do not have
love, I am only a resounding gong or a clanging cymbal.
—1 CORINTHIANS 13:1 (NIV)

As I checked out at the grocery store a while back, I heard a familiar sound: a young child throwing a fit over the injustices befalling him. The offense was that his mother was not buying him a toy when he expected one, and he refused to leave the store until she did. He looked very angry. He looked to be about three years old, maybe four. He also looked to be very much in charge of his mother. I say this because he was standing at one set of doors of the building while his mother stood at the other end of the store in front of the other set, and they were screaming at one another.

Oh, I wish I was kidding right now.

Now, I grocery shop for seven very hungry eaters. This means I buy a lot of food. This means I take a while to check out. These two were screaming when I got up to the counter, and they continued screaming until I walked out of the store. At this point I haven't been back to that store, so for all I know, they are still yelling.

> Kid: Mom. No! I want a toy.
> Mom: No! No! I am leaving. I am not buying you *anything*!

Kid: Mo-o-m! Buy me a toy. I won't leave unless you do.
Mom: Goodbye. I am leaving. [Only she doesn't.] You can just
    stay here!
Kid: Mom! No! [And on and on and on.]

This mom and son were attempting to break one another. And this wasn't these clowns' first rodeo. She had obviously used this break-him-down, wear-him-out parenting tactic for the whole of his three years on this earth, and he was already calling her bluff.

Her sandy-foundation parenting tactics were faltering because they are weakly built. This is really an example of survival of the fittest, but unfortunately for this mother, three-year-olds seem capable of holding on *forever*. Like the Energizer Bunny on uppers, this kid will outlast this mother in fight, *If he plays his cards right, he will be filibustering in Washington when he is grown, but right now he needs to focus. He needs this toy.* longevity, and sheer will to carry on. These two have not established who is boss.

Speak Up with a Quiet Heart

If we were to visit this family at home, we would probably see Mom busy with television or the internet or her phone while Junior misbehaves just out of her reach. Mom might tell him to stop, but chances are she rarely stops what she is doing to deal with him. She probably doesn't normally scream at him quite like this. And she is not yelling for this kid's benefit. She is yelling so every person in the store can see how firm she is as a parent. Somewhere along the way, she was told (or shown) that effective parenting means being the loudest for the longest amount of time. This couldn't be further from the truth. The truth is, the adult yelling, wagging her finger, and stomping her foot is throwing a tantrum too.

Oh, didn't you know that adults threw tantrums? How about whining? I have done it. My son will use his weird, high-pitched whine when he feels the conversation is about to turn against him, and the space-time continuum kicks in while aliens take over my mouth. Sometimes half of our conversation is over before I realize we are both whining at one another.

I don't want to be this guy. I want to just say it. Not offended. Not with a full laying-it-on-pretty-thick secret sermon written between the lines. I want to be more like Jesus, because I am, after all, created in his image. And I am pretty certain he has never been a whiner.

Jesus is the example we turn to for everything, and although he was never an earthly father, I think it's generally accepted that he did an enormous amount of correcting in his lifetime. When the Lord warned Peter that Peter was going to turn his back on Jesus, he said it as a matter of fact, not in the form of a tantrum, and there was certainly no whining (Matt. 26:34).

I am so thankful that God doesn't stand at the other end of the grocery store and yell at me for all to hear. Instead he gets really close, so close no one else is aware, and he whispers into my heart. He just drops an idea into my thoughts.

His voice loves. His words come off the page in Scripture like a love letter.

He is so kind. He shares his wisdom and invites me along to grow through teachings and his words. He never insists. He asks questions that allow me to self-correct. And when I don't quite choose what is right, he holds me while I suffer the natural consequences brought about by my stubborn choices. This is precisely how we should discipline our children, and this leads us to our second form of discipline.

Natural Consequences

Speaking of natural consequences, let's visit this topic for a minute. This method of correction comes from the Big Guy himself. I attribute it to God's love of order. Cause and effect is a real part of disciplining that parents must learn to navigate. If we don't, the costs could be devastating. Our children will find themselves the victim of an enabling parent. Let me paint you a picture you may have already seen lived out in your life on some level.

My oldest child, Izzy, was two years old once and was usually a fairly compliant kid. Her biggest offenses were whining and the occasional bull-headed rebellion. This particular day, she awoke on the alternate, feisty side of the bed, and my husband and his mother were there to witness it.

> Rather than being yelled at for something I knew was wrong, my punishment was quality time with my mom. This family time was what I was really needing anyway, I just didn't know how to ask for it. —Izzy, 20, Missionary kid

In her little wild-child way, Izzy directly disobeyed my husband, so he placed her in time-out. Two minutes of sheer torture: nose to the wall, no sitting, no leaning, no talking, no moving. We may as well have cut off her arms for all the noise she was making. I was proud of my husband. He was standing firm and making her stay in time-out.

This was a major accomplishment because during the last few months I'd caught him "rescuing" her from my enforced consequences. Without meaning to, he was undermining my authority with her because it made him sad to see her suffer. Moreover, he was creating a wedge between my daughter and me. Only he didn't see it. I wasn't able to make him understand. Until his mom came to town.

About one minute into Izzy's time-out, Michael's mom came over and rescued Izzy from her little toddler prison. She hugged her and murmured in her ear that it was OK, and she could be all done. Then my husband's eyes popped out of their sockets and his jaw fell into his lap. I can neither confirm nor deny whether laughter came out of my mouth at the sight of his face. He didn't mince his next words.

"No. No. No. I put her in time-out because she was disobedient, and she knew she was being disobedient. She has to stand there for two minutes, and I am the only one who gets to tell her she is finished. Please don't do that again. We want her to learn."

Then he gave me a sideways glance to see if I was paying attention. Later he apologized to me, and that was the end of that. He stopped enabling my daughter by reinforcing her bad behavior and began allowing her *Oh, the state of my eyebrows at that man!* to reap the consequences of her choices. Incidentally, my mother-in-law can now be heard disciplining my children with a firm but loving, "Um. No." when they get out of hand. They listen and respect her for it.

I realize this is a simple example of a major problem we face as parents, but I look at this blatant disobedience as a gateway drug. If we enable in the simple situations because we are too uncomfortable to follow through, how can we expect to stand by our children when the stakes are very high and the circumstance is extremely awkward? What happens *Seriously. It's that serious.* when we are so angry because we find out our child was the bully, or has been drinking, or got caught lying? Our role as parents is to stand beside our kids in prayer and love at the time of reaping.

Here is another incident in which I had to choose to let my son stand on his own two feet and learn a lesson of reaping what he sowed. One of my boys is brilliant with words. Well, he isn't, but he is going to be once he learns the difference between funny and rude. He is usually a well-liked kid, but he is in sixth grade now, and he seems to struggle when using a filter for his words, so he just doesn't.

He thinks it's amusing to repeat what you have said except that he applies that description to your face. Example: I say, "This shirt is sort of ugly." He says, "Your face is sort of ugly." Hmmm. I see how in his mind it seemed funny. Last time he used it, it seemed to work.

Example: I say, "This car smells like beef and cheese." He replies, "Your face smells like beef and cheese."

OK, maybe his humor is an acquired taste, but the first time I laughed. It was rude, though, and after that, it was no longer funny. His school friends were tired of it, and his teacher asked what I wanted to do about it.

I said let it ride. I agreed to talk to him, but I encouraged her to give her students permission to speak their mind to him. He needs to hear from others, not just me, that his words are harsh and not as funny as he intended. He needs to feel uncomfortable in front of his female friends as they confess that their feelings are hurt because he jokingly said they are fat. He needs to squirm under that positive peer pressure from classmates who don't agree that he must add a sarcastic quip after everything they say. He needs to realize words, not sarcasm, are his spiritual gift. My role as parent in this scenario is different.

I cannot make excuses to the principal, the parents, and the children at school for my kid because he is a bully, which is essentially how his friends were taking him. Because what's to stop his behavior from continuing? Am I going to have to speak to his professors, his boss, and other authorities in his life forever? I can't shield my son from the consequences of his words. However, I can remind him to speak in love, to think about what he is saying before he speaks, to consider what his friends have said to him, and to not repeat his behavior.

Most importantly, I can convey to him that if he isn't obeying 1 Thessalonians 5:11 and building up others with his words, he is disobeying it. He has to decide if he is willing to disobey the Bible in order to be the funny guy. Then, I come back with praise just as Paul did. I tell him when I see him trying and succeeding.

Consequences—Natural, Perks, or Punishments

Most would consider what my parents called punishments to be perks. Once, when I was in high school, a friend told me she needed to go buy pants. I didn't realize she used air quotes in her mind when she said "buy." She was a girl from a rough background whose foremost dream in life was to be in a gang. No kidding. Vegas will do that to a kid.

Her name is Jenny. She dressed like a thug in Dickie shorts complete with gang swag bandana. She tagged on every flat surface she walked near. She cussed like a sailor and threatened old people if they got too close to her. Up to this point, she was the craziest person I ever met. She had taken to me, for some reason, the first time we met down at our neighborhood park. And ever the optimist, I saw potential in *This bit about the elderly might be an exaggeration, but the rest is pretty spot on.* that girl. I needed her to know God loved her even through her junk. She needed me to know my belief in her mattered.

I drove and she didn't, so I agreed to take her to Kmart to get her shopping done. And then she stole a pair of pants. Shoved those guys right down the front of her trousers. Then, in true rebel fashion, she mumbled, "Let's roll." I was stunned and didn't have a clue what to say, so I began rolling. Right into the hands of an undercover security guard, who rolled us promptly to the manager's office.

⁓

Punishment is one of those words that means different things to different people based on their backgrounds. When my husband and I began dating, we talked about how our families handled arguments. In my house, it meant excited debates about topics that rarely mattered. We were pseudolawyers pleading our case over questions such as which way the toilet paper roll should face, why the Cowboys have a stronger defensive line than the Steelers, or what would happen if all the erasers in the world suddenly disappeared. This was our version of fighting, even though fists were never involved. It never occurred to me that others might see it differently. Punishment was hardly ever the outcome to an argument in our family; arguing was fun.

Michael's family arguments were rarely as light. He has witnessed physical interaction that most would call abuse. He wasn't as free to disagree just for the sake of argument. This is when I learned that every home views arguing, punishments, and consequences differently. Some households wouldn't even put these three in the same category.

A punishment is something you earn for being disobedient; a consequence is something that naturally follows a poor decision. In some homes, only the natural consequences matter, and everyone is free to move on. In other homes, punishment and consequence are interchangeable, and if the natural consequence didn't seem to hurt enough, the parents might throw in a punishment of being grounded for good measure. In my family, growing up, punishments were pretty minor compared to the average home.

~

As I sat in that manager's office at Kmart, I felt nervous, anxious, disappointed in myself, and worried that my dad would be disappointed in me too. But I never really worried about a punishment because those were always determined by what would help me learn from my situation and keep me from repeating the action.

My dad came to get us, and since Jenny's parents laid no claim to her when the store called, my dad agreed to take responsibility for her as well. For my punishment, my wise father allowed the cops to lay into me while Jenny kept up an impressive string of eye rolling. My lip quivered through the whole thing.

For Jenny's punishment, my dad took us to the movies. Disney's *Lion King* had just come out in theaters. He bought us popcorn and drinks and candy. I was only seventeen, but I knew what he was doing.

He was forgiving me and reminding me where I come from. And he was loving her in a way no father had ever done for her before. It was her turn for popped-out eyes. Her lip quivered for the whole thing, even though she was a wannabe gang member and seventeen years old. As we made our way to the parking lot, she genuinely apologized to us both.

That day, my father made that little girl see herself differently. He didn't break either of us. He didn't need to. He was brilliant in that moment, and she and I both knew it. Honestly, I knew even then that my father was terrified of my relationship with her. But she needed Jesus, and I had him.

Jenny moved in with us for a while, and I would love to say she became an amazing woman after God's own heart, but I just don't know. I left for college, and she moved back in with her parents for a while, and that was the end of our relationship. I ran into her about five years later, and she was completely drunk at the bar of the restaurant where my going-away party was taking place.

About twenty guests were in attendance. Jenny took the time to talk to each one individually and retell the story of stealing pants and going to the movies. Some of my guests felt uncomfortable—they didn't quite come from where we came from. But I could see she was still overflowing with how much my father had built her up instead of the usual beat-down.

Think About Your Endgame

Punishments aren't meant to pummel kids into the ground so they feel small and stupid, so they wouldn't dare talk by the time we get done with them. We need to try to be the most loving, not the most right, right? The outcome should be lessons learned, relationships strengthened, courses corrected. Our pride should never even enter the picture when we are disciplining, lest our offenses become greater than the crime itself.

I used to think I grew up in a typical household, discipline-wise. As an adult, I can look and see my parents were somewhat oddballs. Loveable oddballs. One thing they did was assign punishments in love, with right intentions, to fit the crime. And that's the point.

10

Join the Club: Mom's Oxygen Mask

He tends his flock like a shepherd:
He gathers the lambs in his arms
and carries them close to his heart;
he gently leads those that have young.
—ISAIAH 40:11 (NIV)

*Y*ou may have heard it said that our relationship with God, and the life we lead, should be handled more like a marathon race than a quick sprint. This analogy works well for us as mothers too, because it allows us time to course-correct when we veer off the path. But before we even get to the race, there are steps we take as mothers to prepare ourselves, and there is maintenance along the way. After all, even if you have the best trainers, a comprehensive training schedule, and the most efficient diet, if you neglect to drink water or take in sustenance during the race, you'll go down like a brick miles before that finish line.

Well, except for me, really, on account of how much I seriously dislike running.

Marathon Mom

We have talked about starting as early as possible with our children to raise them up to be men and women of God. Mama, we need to prepare and train daily if we ever expect to gain mileage in this raising-kids race. We need to find the right running partners who encourage us toward worthwhile paths.

You know what is universal in motherhood? We get tired. Profound, right? I am sure my Pulitzer is being engraved as we speak. In every country, every city, every neighborhood, every situation, mothers get tired and need more comfort than mere humans can provide.

In 2 Corinthians 1, we get some very good news. The God of all comfort wants to draw us in, fill us with his grace and peace and patience, and love us so genuinely that we can't help but pay some of that forward (vv. 3–5). In return for these precious gifts, God asks us to do unto others as he is doing for us. In short, we get filled so we can pour out. I know this topic can feel a little risky, but this chapter focuses on the filling up more than on the pouring out.

The Balance in Your Break

We all have different activities that feed our souls. We have to take the time to pick the best for ourselves and go for it. Feed away. Soak it up. But be concise and purposeful. Above all, be balanced. This tightrope between mom-refuel-time and (I am just going to call it what it is) neglecting our families is a precarious road to travel.

Our mission seems obvious. We just want a few hours of speaking frankly with another mom instead of in toddler code. Maybe an entire dinner where we aren't sharing food or picking up the spoon our little angel insists on throwing to the ground every ten minutes. How about some time to just sit in the sunshine with a book without ever needing to look up? Sometimes I just want to be alone in the quiet of my own home and have the silence not signal the disfiguring of all of my most favorite owl figurines with a permanent marker. Somewhere along the way, the temptation to just keep resting or taking that break stops being a rare occurrence and is now the new

Or every two minutes. Whichever comes first.

normal. Our training schedule gets out of whack. Let's take a look, shall we?

Marathon Training Plan

No matter who your trainer is and the length or type of race you attempt, a few foundational elements apply to training for something physical. In mothering, we train physically, spiritually, and emotionally. First you need a plan. A narrowed-down, focused plan.

Raise your hand if you like to run. See me next to you with my hand down? Yah, well, I found a T-shirt that reads, "I don't run, and if you see me running, you should run too because it means a bear is chasing me." I found another one that says, "I run. Just kidding, I take naps."

You can put your hands down now. I'll never fully understand your love for this activity, but you can bet that I totally understand *why* you do it. This is what feeds your soul. And I am so happy that you found it. I found a few things of my own: photography and scrapbooking, reading, and watching baseball.

These feed my soul. For you it may be baking, cleaning and organizing, rafting, sewing, hiking, working on cars, exercising, gardening, bird watching, building, home decorating, collecting figurines, or watching sports. I like some of these some of the time, but I have narrowed down what authentically fills me up with the *If it's organizing, please just come to my house. I need you.* mental and emotional energy to pour out for others. Because let's face it, as mothers we pour. And pour.

And pour.

And pour some more.

And then, when we see the end of the day in sight, and we get what no one would call a second wind and manage to make it upstairs into our beds with most of our teeth loosely brushed over, something happens and we get asked to pour out yet again.

"Mommy, my sock fell off."

Soul Care

What feeds your soul? What helps you forget the daily grind for a few minutes a week? Write it down. Right here. Just doodle it in the margin. Write everything that comes to your mind, and then begin to narrow down the field based on your budget, your schedule, your resources, and basically what makes you smile for a while.

My list was so long I'd have to live to be a thousand in order to really enjoy any of it properly. I took a look at the things that help me decompress and face the next task at hand, and then I tossed the activities that should have been relaxing but felt like work. Maybe they are relaxing to someone else, but not me. I simplified my list to just a few of my favorites. I decorate my home with photos of my family: photography. What about all the rest of those pictures? Scrapbooking. I love learning and am a fan of teen literature: reading. I also have a strong love for movies and sarcasm, which I squeeze in at any chance I can.

I recommend everyone try this. So let's do it. Let's make that list and narrow it down.

Maybe you are that mom who has been so wrapped up in her kids that she no longer knows who she is or what on earth she wants anymore. It's time to find *you* again. Don't feel guilty about this. God wants you to know you again too. You need to find something that frees you up from whatever threatens to push you down. "Where the Spirit of the Lord is, there is freedom" (2 Cor. 3:17 NIV). Since the Spirit dwells in each believer, you and I have freedom in our very beings.

What I am saying is, do something edifying. Since God has called you to be a mama, he will fill you up with everything you need if you let him. We know that God gives a little extra love to those who tend his flock. He hunkers down with us and restores what we have poured out. Isaiah 40:11 reminds us that "he tends his flock like a shepherd: He gathers the lambs in his arms and carries them close to his heart; he gently leads those that have young" (NIV). As we do this with our babies, God does it with us.

In taking the time to reset, you allow space for God to refill you spiritually. You shove off all that struggle and trade in the chaos for peace that surpasses human understanding. Spiritual renewing isn't limited to reading the Bible or memorizing Scripture. It sure can include that, but God delights in our entire selves.

The Bible is full of stories of people who embraced this idea of spiritual renewing. Esther was a dinner hostess. David was a musician. Ruth spent face time with her mother-in-law. Esau was a hunter. Adam was a farmer. Joseph was a talented businessman. Moses found peace on a mountainside tending his sheep. Paul found joy in sharing Christ with anyone and everyone. Jesus took naps.

When David says, "Take delight in the LORD, and he will give you the desires of your heart" (Ps. 37:4 NIV), he means these things. These things that renew us so we can turn around and

I believe we should all do this in remembrance of him. Amen.

resume being that Missionary Mama we pray to become. This marathon work laid before us as mothers.

David continues in Psalm 37 to explain that in doing these things—these heart desires that glorify God—we begin to shine: "Commit everything you do to the LORD. Trust him, and he will help you. He will make your innocence radiate like the dawn, and the justice of your cause will shine like the noonday sun" (vv. 5–6). Later, in Philippians 2, we are told to shine brightly for Christ: "For God is working in you, giving you the desire and the power to do what pleases him" (v. 13).

Isn't that exactly what this renewing is meant to do? Are you beginning to see that God cares for the whole you? He wants to take everything you do—even the minutes you might count as self-focused—and turn them into something he can use. If you're tired and cranky and hungry (for both real and spiritual food), what you are putting out there for others stinks. Sometimes literally. However, when you take the time to express your talents through things you love to do, you refresh yourself so that you can shine the way God intends.

"Since God chose you to be the holy people he loves, you must clothe yourselves with tenderhearted mercy, kindness, humility, gentleness, and patience" (Col. 3:12). If we set ourselves up to function in this pattern of filling up according to the desires God imparts *before* we pour out to our children and others in our ministry of daily life, we are left with glorious results. Not only are we truly renewed, but those around us sense Jesus in us; we can't help but shine out his glory everywhere we go, even in the most stressful situations.

Let's Get Together

Being a missionary isn't what it used to be. Or rather, I don't think it's what we've made it to be. Jesus healed and walked beside and ate with and laughed with and wept over and offered an outstretched hand. That's it. That's being a missionary. It happens right here, and over there, and wherever you are. It looks a lot of ways and usually includes others.

Sometimes it's inviting people to church, but that often feels weird, and there's a reason. I haven't looked it up, but I don't think Jesus ever invited someone to a building. Being a missionary Jesus-style simply means inviting people into our lives and sharing life with them. All of it. No limit. It's the smallest and biggest thing you'll ever do all at once. It's messy and takes us out of our comfort zone, but while sometimes God asks us to minister to our kids, at other times he wants us to partner up with other moms in the trenches.

We aren't meant to do this gig alone. And insisting on doing it alone only gives the enemy the space he needs to get you thinking your house is the only house who has it this bad. Your kids are the only kids who act this way. You are the only one hurting because of your children. Those are lies that are magnified in isolation.

Trust me when I say that each of my girls, around the age of twelve or thirteen, woke up one morning as if a beast had taken over her face and a lesser demon had attached itself to her voice box. It was brutal, and I prayed and disciplined them as much as was needed while my husband researched psychiatrists, certain our daughters needed serious mental intervention. I called my mom friends in a panic.

My Ten Basic Needs
- Laughter
- Understanding
- Validation
- Attention
- Affection
- Sex
- Space
- Freedom

(I can't think of anything else right now.)
—Melissa, Missionary Mom of two

A week later, all was right again. They started their periods just like every other girl in history, and we found our sweet girls again.

If I didn't have other mamas around me to warn me how normal this was, I might have joined my husband in finding a temporary psychiatric ward. Turns out that thirteen-year-olds with PMS have moments of irrationality. I say this in jest, but I am not kidding at all when I say my husband was truly worried that they needed intervention. We both breathed a sigh of relief after consulting the other moms. Being a parent is a club sport. We can't and shouldn't do it alone.

Embrace Your Vert

I know that some of you are cringing at the idea of joining others in parenting on a regular basis. After thirty-eight seconds of meeting me you'll know I am obviously an extrovert. It fills my heart to be with others and talk to others. I don't actually like being alone. Ever. I don't always need to talk with someone, but I am absolutely an extrovert. This means parenting with others sounds like the best idea ever.

Many of you are thinking that parenting in a village format seems just fine if you can also have a little time alone. You love the idea of the support, but maybe you renew best when you are alone. This split style is known as "ambivert." It means you can be on when it's time to be on. You can lead a training, you can chat it up with a group of other moms, and you are happy to offer advice to a group of new Missionary Moms. It also means you need a few days to decompress after you've put yourself out there so far. Being alone after that show of extroversion will give you the processing time you need in order to stick your neck out there again the next time you are called to lead.

Some of you are introverts. The idea of partnering with others to raise kids and to refuel sounds counter to what fills you up. You like the quiet. You need your alone time. Standing out in the group to give advice or lead in some way sounds like asking to be punched in the face and given an anxiety attack. This is OK too.

To each of you I say, embrace your "vert." *This should be on a T-shirt.* God has created you to be a Missionary Mom in a way that is completely unique to you. I am not called to wear your vert and parent your kids. And vice versa. But we need each other. I need you to teach me how to balance my vert and reassure me that my kids aren't crazy or failing. And maybe you need to see how I speak to my kids or feel encouraged that I will be there when you need a shoulder to cry on. We are all works in progress. By coming together to lead our children in community, we set ourselves up for the best success in parenting. With God at the center of our group, there is no more room for fear, doubt, or anything else the enemy wants to plant.

11

It Takes a Villager

In everything set them an example by doing what is good. In your teaching show integrity, seriousness and soundness of speech that cannot be condemned, so that those who oppose you may be ashamed because they have nothing bad to say about us.
—TITUS 2:7–8 (NIV)

$\mathcal{S}$tart early,
choose faith,
pray for every person to whom God introduces you,
worship,
be in fellowship with others,
find accountability,
be aware of others.
Be a member of the Village People!
Wait. What? No, I don't mean that kind of villager.

Think more community helper and less YMCA.

Those Are Your Kids Too

Being a villager means you are invested in your kid and all the kids God puts around you. Yet I wish I had a dollar for every time one of us thought, "I like my kids; I just don't like other people's kids." I've thought it myself at times, and I've heard it said so. many. times. It is like so many other things the enemy whispers into our hearts. Rather than see them as lies, we believe his words.

Accepting these words keeps us from being a villager to kids—ours and everyone else's—who might need what we have to offer.

We aren't meant to internalize lies. We are meant to meditate on God's Word, so his truths become a part of us. God says, "Keep this Book of the Law always on your lips; meditate on it day and night, so that you may be careful to do everything written in it. Then you will be prosperous and successful" (Josh. 1:8 NIV).

When we convince ourselves that we are no good at leading or loving other people's kids, we set up boundaries and tell God, "I love you, but I will only obey you in this space, in this way, and with these people." When Joshua stood before his people and said greatness awaited them on the other shore of the Jordan River, they didn't look at him and say, "Look. We love God and we respect you. But you're crazy if you think we're gonna cross that river. We like people, but we're good here. We will just stay here in this spot and wait for God to do something with all this."

Nope.

They said, "We will do whatever you command us, and we will go wherever you send us" (v. 16). It was heavy, this promise. They followed it up with, "Anyone who rebels against your orders and does not obey your words and everything you command will be put to death" (v. 18). I am not suggesting that we turn this into a martyr situation, but the point is the same. Saying yes to being God's villager means something. To you, to other parents, and to those kids.

You are a missionary by choice, God's choice. Also, you have free will. You could take this book and all its finest nonsense and chuck it across the room. Stick it in the fireplace. Throw it off a mile-long bridge. Run it over with your car and stick it in the freezer with your copy of *The Shining*.

But closing these pages doesn't change the fact that you may be the first example of Jesus the kids in your neighborhood will see. You are working on purpose to be a mother after God's own heart. I challenge you to lose this idea of only liking your children and replace it with God's intentions for you. And them.

You Could Be a History Teacher

We are beginning to understand that God wants us to teach our children to live intentionally, never letting go of their biblical history. Throughout the Bible, God tells parents to teach their children of his promises, his faithfulness. He says, "These commandments that I give you today are to be on your hearts. Impress them on your children" (Deut. 6:6–7 NIV). We can no longer sit idly by and watch children flounder in the streets because they have no one to "impress" upon them. Just when you think they have no one to tell them about the biblical greats who have come before them, please realize they have someone. They have *you*. God made *you* their neighbor.

Of course, you get to decide how you will define the word "neighbor," but Dictionary.com says it simply: a fellow human being. Did you just make a face?

Did someone who sort of annoys you just pop into your mind, and then you made a face because you don't really like to think of them as a fellow human being? That would be admitting you have something in common.

Well. You do.

Both of you are human beings, created in the image of the most loveable and understanding God. And both of you are also people who crave love and acceptance.

People are not easy to love. Oh, wait. I am a people. You are a people. Then it stands to reason that we are not easy to love.

Take a minute right now and remember yourself in your meanest and most obnoxious times. Jot it all down right here as an in-the-margins confession. Then let's say this quick prayer together.

Lord, I confess that I don't love the way I should when you put tough people in front of me. I also admit that I forget that I myself am difficult to love. I don't want to come across as superior. Show me when this is my attitude and replace it with a heart that wants only to be a light for you. Then bring them, Lord. Bring whoever you want. Let me accept your mercy and grace so I am better able to pour them out on others. Amen.

Now think of a few people God put in your life who loved you anyway, and say a prayer for them. I can remember specific moments when I said the most ridiculous thing and behaved like a twit, only to be loved by a youth leader or my best friend's mom or a neighbor lady. Kids go through it probably a lot more than you might think. We can't hand over to others the opportunities God puts before us, especially at the tail end of praying for God to use us. It's like asking for a once-in-a-lifetime chance, and then when God hands it to us, we reject it because it doesn't fit our comfy parameters.

When Sam was little, we would make reasonable requests of him, and he would try to kindly decline. He felt if he was respectful while he rejected us, it was fine. I would say, "Can you please go clean up your room?" And because he was smart for a four-year-old, he would politely respond with a "No, thank you." He was calm and spoke with zero sarcasm.

Opting out, even with manners, is still saying "no."

Don't Wash Your Hands of This

When we ask God for something and then opt out of the opportunities he brings to us, we are living a tiresome, cyclical life. We are missing out on the blessing that comes with first-time obedience. We can see how this lifestyle plays out when we look back in the Bible to Joshua and the Israelites. The Israelites had wandered in the desert for forty years praying that God would give them a place of their own—a land to dwell in. And God answered. We pick up in Joshua chapter six where God asked the Israelites to obey in crazy ways. God said march around the wall of Jericho every day for seven days and don't say anything. And they did. He said blow some horns and shout so the wall will fall. They did.

And in the miraculous way that only God could manage, the walls of Jericho came crashing to the ground. Then God gave the Israelites clear steps to take to conquer those inside the rubble. Step by step they were to follow, "but Israel violated the instructions about the things set apart for the LORD" (7:1). They asked. God answered. And they said, "No, thank you" with their actions, because the deal wasn't quite what they had in mind.

It seems to me as if God includes this portion of Scripture to show us the ramifications of the Israelites' actions. So let's take this as a warning from God that if we hear his direction and choose to take matters into our own hands, no one wins. Even if we have obeyed everything up to this point, there will be serious ramifications if we disobey.

Even after all of their obedience to what are arguably some odd requests on God's part, the Israelites lost God's favor. Over greed. Their conversation went something like this:

> God: Obey all this. Even the far-fetched bits. The harvest will be great, I promise.
> Israelites: Yes. Yes. Yes. Yes. This is interesting, but yes. And, no thank you.

We do this. I did it yesterday. I don't mean I stole riches and doomed my entire nation. But I find I function in this pattern in a steady cycle of obey/disobey even when I don't want to. I'll take dinner to someone who needs a hand. I'll give a dollar to a homeless guy for a coffee. I say yes all the way until things get too uncomfortable. Sometimes I even say yes to the craziest things, just like the Israelites did. But then I revert to my self-focused needs and ignore the needs of those who God puts around me.

We say "No, thank you" to God when he puts a mom, kid, elderly man, or some other neighbor in our path and we opt out. No amount of manners will make this response a good one. We'll never be perfect in our responses to God's provision, but making a concerted effort to say "Yes, Lord" can go a long way.

Parental Guidance Suggested

We are surrounded by kids in our neighborhood. But even if you only have one neighbor kid in addition to your own child, there is bound to be a mama nearby. My whole dream in life is to get to our youth through their mamas. It looks a lot of ways, but my reach will be different from yours because we are different people.

We have unique talents and desires. I have a love for baseball that some moms may not care about. I also have the ability to sense when a movie quote needs to be added to everyday conversation. If another mom laughs and names that movie, we become best friends. She doesn't have a choice. We are a rare breed, so when we find one another; it's like that scene when Anne with an E meets Diana Barry, and we must be friends forever.

> My youth pastor was the first person I felt believed that I could have an impact on this world. —Aurora, 23, Missionary kid

Our lights are different, but they each point to the same Jesus. So don't limit yourself in thinking God only intends to make you a villager for the kids. Chances are, if you live near children, God is asking you to stand with their mamas as well.

The whole idea of loving alongside your neighbor may seem foreign to you. And once you accept it, it's going to seem crazy to the people around you. They'll get over it. Being this bold and asking for this much face-to-face time might be awkward, because we are so used to pulling into our garages and walking into our houses without ever making eye contact with others. But it just takes a little Holy Spirit to smooth out the awkward vibe. If we are faithful to stick with it even when it's uncomfortable, then the Finisher of our faith will begin to reveal that this fight is worth it. You simply have to believe that love is worth fighting for.

12

Who Are Your Villagers?

I always thank my God when I pray for you.
—PHILEMON 1:4

*C*hapter 10 had us thinking about ways we spend our time that fill us up in our minds and hearts. You were challenged with finding hobbies that celebrate your God-given gifts and interests, and you were granted permission to seek out other mothers (or embrace your need to be introverted) to unwind from your heavy load of being a Missionary Mom. This chapter looks a little more closely into what God says about being filled spiritually and how that rolls seamlessly into filling others. We have an idea who our neighbors are, but have you ever stopped to ask, "Who are *my* people?" You aren't only called to pour out to others; you also need to be poured into, and that requires living in community.

We Do This on Purpose Too

Forging connection won't happen by accident. Some relationships will grow organically, others might require a more piecemeal approach, and sometimes you will simply have to force the matter. In any case, you cannot live a life that only empties. Pretty soon you'd be so hollow that you'd have nothing to offer those around you.

So let's consult one of the most iconic layouts of what a balanced life of pouring out and being filled looks like: the book of Titus.

Paul opens his letter to Titus with a reminder of Paul's calling: "To proclaim faith to those God has chosen and to teach them to know the truth that shows them how to live godly lives" (Titus 1:1). The whole purpose of his letter is to encourage Titus and his people and to lay out the framework of how a village is supposed to function.

Paul tells us who leaders are to be and what to look for in a mentor. He throws out goal-worthy words like faithful, manager, blameless, honest, slow to anger, hospitable, devout, disciplined, strong belief, encouraging, and more (vv. 6–9). Paul isn't writing about being perfect. He's writing about what church elders should strive for. And as we come under the wisdom and direction of older (and spiritually wiser) churched women who chase after these characteristics, we not only benefit from their example, but we also get to reap what they are sowing out over us.

Note to self and every mom everywhere: Get yourself a good mentor. You might have to ask the outright question, "Will you be my mentor?" Don't be shy. She will love being asked.

Discipleship between women is arguably the most precious gift and one of the enemy's most hated forms of love, maybe second only to the love found in marriage. According to an article in *Psychology Today* magazine, there are seven types of love found in the Greek language.[5] Six of those seven are represented in marriage. That's a whole lot of love! Between us girls, we want to see four: agape, philia, ludus, and pragma.

Agape	Unconditional love: without limits or expectation
Philia	Deep friendship: loyal and sacrificial love, willing to fight on behalf of the loved one (maybe literally)

Ludus	Playful love: banter over coffee
Pragma	Longstanding love: the kind that knows how to compromise and yield in a healthy way

We all need a little of these types of love poured into us on a steady basis. Paul writes, "Older women must train the younger women to love their husbands and their children, to live wisely and be pure, to work in their homes, to do good, and to be submissive to their husbands. Then they will not bring shame on the word of God" (Titus 2:4–5).

No pressure, ladies. Paul is just saying we have the opportunity to either stand out in the name of Christ's love or tarnish the very Word of God. We need you. I need you.

#nbd

I am guessing you just read that verse and thought, "Yes, I need those older moms. Gimme, gimme, fill me up!" Now stop and consider that you might just be someone else's older mom.

Look Both Ways

Please don't slap me. I didn't say you're old. I merely think we don't always realize when we need to roll over from being the served to being the server. "All of life and ministry is to be lived in light of this tension between who we *already* are in Christ and who we *hope* to someday be."[6] It's a constant shift really, because at any point we are older than someone and younger than someone else.

Age is just a number. Where we land on this hierarchy of loving other moms comes from the experience we have lived as women. If you are older than the girl next to you, then Titus two is referring to you. At the same time, if you are younger than the lady next to you, then you should work on that relationship. We need to look in both directions to know our role in any given relationship. The way we interact in these relationships can look many different ways.

Recently I listened to a podcast about how a few women brought this very idea into the twenty-first century and put more than hands and feet to a ministry. Cindy Berglund, Stephanie Armstrong, and Laura Ludvigson run a women's ministry called Authentic Pursuit/ Titus 2 Mentoring. The group focuses solely on partnering women in mentor/mentee relationships. Their goals resonated with me as someone needing the service they were offering. As I learned more about their group, I could easily imagine myself passing this sort of support on to the younger women around me.

In a world where social media seems to separate us more than unite us, and in the face of the plan of the enemy—namely, to make us each feel like island life is the only way—these ladies teach that none of us need to live alone. It all began because they saw the younger generation not just leaving the church but fleeing in droves. They dared to ask the question "Why?" They talked a lot about the millennial generation, but I felt like they were reading my story too.

> I really enjoy mentoring new moms. It is such an exciting and scary time. I wish I had someone when I was a new mom.
> —Mindy, Missionary Mom of three

I want to be mentored. In fact, I need it. I want to walk alongside someone who is rooting for me and willing to cry with me when I'm not seeing clearly. When I can't make sense of Scripture, I need someone to share her wisdom over it all. More than anything, I need someone to keep pointing me toward Jesus. Am I alone in this, or are you too raising your hand and saying, "Sign me up!"

Spiritual mentoring is about aligning ourselves with wise women in our churches and communities who call us into maturity in Christ. Stephanie Armstrong stated, "As we mentor the next generation, it's not just that we want to pass on our great ideas, or that we want to even share the wisdom we have. No, we really want to call them to maturity in Christ."[7] If I am honest, I am begging for this sort of accountability, yet I am also terrified of it. But I know in my guts that it's right. This is how God meant it. You pouring into me, me pouring into her, and her soaking it all in until she too has something to offer. Without godly support, we struggle more than we need to.

Here's the skinny on what this looks like on a day-to-day basis. It's fluid and intertwined with our everyday activities. It isn't simply passing along cooking techniques and DIY lifehacks for an hour each week. It's deeper than that and yet more basic at times. "It's a movement, not a ministry, because it doesn't have a calendar," says Laura Ludvigson.

Sometimes it's eating dinner together or grabbing coffee and talking about what you're each reading in your quiet times. Other times it's knee to knee in prayer or hosting a "momscape" where mamas of littles take turns babysitting because every mom needs the chance to wander around Target kid-free for an hour. Maybe you even work at memorizing Scripture together.

As only God can arrange, the mentoring often begins to go both directions. Laura points out, "You don't know where your mentoring is going to go—the ripple effect—you will lose track of who's mentoring who down the line." This is as it should be. Our relationship with God grows as we begin to be intentional about letting others pour into us. Only once this is a pattern in our life do we begin to see we have something to give back. And it's really quite simple because we've watched this example in the one who's been mentoring us.

Cindy Burglen closed out the podcast episode by saying, "We want purpose and satisfaction in our life. We want joy in our life. We want fulfillment. All of these things in our life. And when we're investing in somebody else—allowing God to invest in us, so we can invest in somebody else—it gives us real joy, purpose, and fulfillment." This is the stuff Missionary Moms are made of.

It's Not a Contest

Relationships we have with other moms should be prodded on by love, not competition as we saw in our two misguided mamas at the park in chapter 4. When I think of the example Jesus set among his disciples, I see more and more that I want to love that way. In the face of pending betrayal, major doubt, and having to repeat himself over and over and over and . . . he still loved. He remained patient and spoke as if that person in front of him was the most important reason for him to be there.

Seriously. It's like we are our own four-year-olds who need to hear the same thing on repeat. He's our number one cheerleader, though. He's totally willing to do it.

Can you imagine what would happen if we treated other moms this way? If, in spite of knowing they might let us down, we worked to instill in them a confidence that nothing is too big to get in the way of our friendship? What if we loved those ladies so big through prayer and actions that they felt comfortable asking for prayer in *anything*, even the messiest bits? How would it feel to know that you could confess your worst parenting moments and know you wouldn't be labeled based on your mistakes? Would you like to be received that way?

I sure would. This ebb and flow of needing that sort of unconditional love and offering it right back because it's what we all need? That's church, my friend. That's the village living we are meant to function in.

New in Town

Some of you might be thinking, "I am new in town," or, "I don't know a single person." You might even be the only woman of your age or nationality, or you might speak a completely different language from everyone else around you. You are thinking that this sort of discipleship sounds really great on paper, but there are too many obstacles for it to really fan out like I've described. To that I say, God knows what you need.

He also knows what you're capable of. So take a good look at your gifts, look at your surroundings, say some serious prayers, and make it happen. Connect with the women around you, whether they are moms or not, and start this movement on your own. Coffee. Tea. Weekly prayer time. Soccer moms' club. Knitting. Scrapbooking. Eating Grapes Club. It doesn't matter what you do.

Open yourself up and welcome some people around you. Invite some people over for tacos. Start a MOPS group at your church. Look back to your list of what feeds your soul and ask some others to join you in it. Begin mentoring some college students, and then go talk to an older woman in your community about mentoring you. What your theme is doesn't matter as much as what your motive is.

If you feel like you are all alone and really need some people, chances are there are other women who feel exactly the same way. Because we aren't meant to do this alone. Not one little bit. Step out and then trust God to bring your village to light. Your people might show up at your door, or you might need to show up at theirs. Moses only had to hold his rod out over the sea for something amazing to take place. You could do that, right?

13

Who Are Your Kids' Village People?

He set my feet on solid ground
and steadied me as I walked along.
He has given me a new song to sing,
a hymn of praise to our God.
Many will see what he has done and be amazed.
They will put their trust in the LORD.
—PSALM 40:2–3

Several times in my life I have hung out with a visitor or friend who speaks with an accent. It takes about a day, but suddenly I too have this accent. And because I am a spaz, it only comes out about every ten words or so. Ever watch Jeopardy? I am like Alex Trebek when he uses a Spanish accent. "The correct answer is *Guatemala*!"

He speaks in his typical American vibe until he gets to that last word, and suddenly he's born and raised in Guatemala City. This too is how I am when I hang out with my Boston friends, my New Zealand friend, my Texas people, or any other friend with *I'm serious, y'all.* an accent. It just becomes my new normal.

I've seen this happen in nearly all human relationships with accents, habits, belief systems, and major and minor stances. I hang out with someone who uses the words "dude," "like," "seriously," or "bruh," and suddenly these are part of my daily vernacular. Like, every other

word, seriously. Dude. It's crazy, dude-bruh. It *It would be great if you could shoot me a note on social media letting me know I am not in this alone.*
just sneaks up on me, and I don't even know I am doing it.

Sometimes this happens over way more serious things. I start hanging out with someone who tends to complain, and I start to complain about things I've never actually cared about previously. I get sucked into new normals easily. It hit me one day that the same thing is happening with American parents as we talk about our kids.

The Power of Life and Death

I've heard it said about seventy-six times this month alone that the existing younger generations are going to amount to nothing. Maybe the language isn't so blatant, but endlessly ranting about how these incoming adults won't work, have no real skills, and only care about their phones is basically saying the same thing.

This diatribe is setting a bar we may regret establishing. And you know what I think has happened? I think one day, not that long ago, the devil whispered this nonsense into someone's ear. He threw out words like "millennial" and "Generation Z" and even gave the definition of who that makes *our* kids.

Several someones. Then I think someone repeated it out of fear or maybe an unguarded heart. They kept saying it until the people they were around suddenly found themselves repeating it as truth. Just like we do when we copy that fancy British accent. It's there before we realize it's happening.

I'm tired of it. Are we really allowing the world to define our children? What is this we are speaking over them? Are we seriously nonchalantly throwing out a, "My kid will probably never move out. She can't even get a job"? This is in direct opposition to our calling as Missionary Moms who speak life over our kids. Kids who are trained up in the way they should go could never fall under this category.

James warns anyone speaking loosely with her tongue, "If you claim to be religious but don't control your tongue, you are fooling yourself, and your religion is worthless" (1:26). He finishes that thought by admonishing us to refuse "to let the world corrupt you" (v. 27). Proverbs reminds us that words have the power of life or death (18:21). We choose.

Lord, let our words draw our children to your heart and not leave them feeling like we follow a foolish religion. Amen.

Mamas, we have the chance as mothers to be the first missionaries our children ever see. We have the honor of being their number one fan, spurring them on through love. Do we want our children to hear us speak encouragement and life over them? Or will we simply keep repeating the enemy's opinion?

Trust me. This is absolutely the enemy's message.

Proverbs 12:6 says, "The words of the wicked are like a murderous ambush, but the words of the godly save lives." I tend to take this word literally. I don't have space enough to include the statistics on how a parent's belief in a child keeps them from drug addiction, promiscuity, alcoholism, and a life apart from Christ. We can look at the prisons to see that absent parents contribute to this system, whereas involved parents who love and speak life over their children change things.

This verse goes so far as to say that godly words save lives. This could be our child's life or someone else's eternal salvation because we've shifted from having a mess of a kid to a mission-minded kid. Just as importantly, we have an opportunity to bring change to our communities and the way they see our children. We should bring that change. And we must. Because these kids didn't just wake up changing the world.

Lean in. Because this is about to get raw. We raised these kids. We. Us. If there is a problem, it is a direct reflection of our parenting.

The Center for Generational Kinetics studies generations. You know who they say has all the power in changing a generation? Parents. "The three key trends that shape generations are parenting, technology, and economics."[8] Parenting is the number one game changer for our children.

So What Are We Gonna Do About It?

The best way to combat the world's view of our kids, and instead turn out kids who chase after Christ with all their guts, is simple. We have to lead our sheep. They need to know our voice, they need to know God's voice, and they need to live their own great calling. Because God has given our children their own village people.

> My uncle, who later became my pastor, was one of my biggest influences as far as doing missions and learning how to go into a community and ask what needs to be done. I also was constantly encouraged by my parents to serve others as we often did outreaches as a family. —Izzy, 20, Missionary kid

They may not intuitively know this, so we get to set the example. We intentionally bring them into new normal. But this time, instead of asking our kids to sit back and watch our idle hands, we ask them to have the constant heart of a servant. This can look a million different ways. The only way it really has to look is humble.

This list of ways our kids can serve is endless. Bring them to work in a soup kitchen on the weekends. Start a notes-of-encouragement group where the kids write thank-you notes to the elderly in your community. They can clean up garbage. Pay for food behind them at the drive-through. Leave a flower on every doorstep you pass on a family walk. Make them aware of the homeless teenagers in your area, and allow them to be creative in how they serve these kids. Volunteer to hang out with foster kids on Friday nights. Serve with kids at church. Go with them on a mission trip.

You might be thinking, "I do a lot of this." This isn't a list for you. This is a list of ways for you to spend time with your kids. Movies, water parks, hours in front of a screen—those are OK, but there's something more intentional you can do to counteract this drivel that's expected of Gen Z.

Be missionaries together. Whatever that looks like. As the Missionary Mom, you get to set the standard that a life that serves others is normal. Average. And it happens right here as part of your mission field.

These activities aren't small. Even the simplest offering from a child radiates through a neighborhood. Do you know why? Because you haven't just taught your kid to serve. You haven't simply given them a job to do or even helped the guy on the receiving end. No. This work is so much mightier than this. You have given your child a voice.

Can You Hear Me Now?

This great big world is so loud it can be crippling. The irony is that the noise and commotion of technology is so deafening that it has caused most of our kids to go silent over everything that matters. The web of interconnectedness on social media has created a black hole of sorts. We don't fully interact with one another. We speak aloud much less. Our bravado has slipped into falsehood where we are often terrified to step up and out and speak up for what we believe.

Nowadays we are mostly only fake brave because social media offers a sense of invisibility. I can say anything I want on there, right? I don't really have to look anyone in the eyes. There's so much less ownership to the relationships we have online compared to what happens when we are face to face. It's time to step out from behind that façade of connection and use the voice and talents and skills and gifts God has given us. This is the example we need to set for our sons and daughters.

Our kids need to know there is no age at which ministry begins. We need them to speak up about what God puts on their hearts. Their story, their words, their ministry. It's time we encourage them to let that out. We can't tell their stories. They must speak up and use the voices God has given them.

Listen to Them—Then Get Them Going

Spend a few minutes talking with a kid. Any kid. Really talking about something that matters. Ask them questions about their struggles and strengths. Ask them where they see a lack of ministry happening in the community. It's amazing what they see. Begin praying together about how to fill that void, and then listen. *Listen to them.* Together listen to God as he reveals how to bridge that gap. Believe in these kids enough to help them take steps. Buy them the resources to do something to help others.

Does a boy want to make sandwiches for homeless teens? Put the word out that you are taking weekly donations of sandwich supplies to help him do just that. Make it a group affair by including the whole Sunday school or youth group. Maybe a young woman wants to start a modest clothing line for teen girls. Sign her up for sewing lessons. Help her research business startup steps. Maybe *your* kids want to feed the community some tacos, just so the teens in their school will have a safe place to come when they are really going through it. Be willing to open your home in a way that makes this easy.

Our kids have everything to offer, and they are eager to do so. It's time for us to rework our conversations about them and teach them the skills they need to reach out for a mentor, seek God in prayer, obey him with audacity, and speak up to tell their own story.

The Perfect Pour

Just as we need others to pour into us so we can pour out, our kids need to learn this balance as well. We get to have a hand in setting it up so it is healthy.

First, we give our babies right back to God. If we have been too heavy-handed and interfered with our kids' voices, we may need to confess our controlling behavior to Christ. He understands. He already knows how great our kids are. And he also cares for them more than we do.

Next, we take our kids to church. Of course, the act of walking into church and attending service means very little on our scale of what makes us heaven bound. But remember, we are prone to shifting our beliefs, our passions, and even our accents depending on who we spend time with. It's no different with our children. If they are surrounded by like-minded Christian kids, their voice will begin to sound a bit louder and a little more like Jesus.

Finally, we teach our kids why it matters to choose their friends wisely. This isn't a one-time lesson. And while a whole lot of it happens at the back end of a bad friend choice, much can be done ahead of time. My favorite time to bring this up is during our car rides. I throw out a question like, "Hey. How did you feel when you saw so-and-so talking all through church tonight?" Or, "What would you do if someone you were hanging out with started talking disrespectfully about a teacher?"

I am not only teaching my child to be ready for the inevitable. I am also giving her permission to speak up when the time comes. Sometimes this is between peers. Others it means speaking up on a peer's behalf.

Teach Them to Submit to Authority (the Right Way)

My daughter's college professor ran a risky exercise. He spent about an hour lecturing the group. "Alright! I am tired of talking so much. How about we mix it up a little for the last part of class. I can tell there's a festival or event happening outside, and I am curious about checking it out. I can't leave, so I am going to choose some of you to head out there. Can I get all the nonwhite students to stand up and head out there? Come back in about twenty minutes and give us an update."

After a few awkward glances between students, the select group departed the class. The professor added, "OK. Let's talk about homework. Why don't you all move to the front of the classroom." He's casually moved all the white kids to the front of the class, knowing the students who returned would find themselves in the back of the class.

Anyone else feeling super uncomfortable with this professor? I think he's brilliant.

The longer my daughter kept telling me this story, the more I began to see his call to action. He was trying to teach these college kids how easily divided they can be from their convictions.

The whole time the first group was gone, he kept talking about their homework, about the video they had watched over the weekend, about anything that could distract them from what was really going on in the class. My daughter spoke up and threw out a "This is weird. What's going on?"

The professor responded, "Izzy, can't we just talk about the homework?"

Seeing that no one else was speaking up, she waited to see if anyone else would jump in with her. When the students returned, one young man noticed the separation and moved up front, but he said nothing. My daughter sat with an angsty teen face, annoyed at everyone, then asked again, "What's going on here?"

"I'll tell you," the professor added, and continued after a pregnant pause. "You allowed me to segregate you. And really easily too." The students spent the rest of the class feeling offended that the whole thing had been a diversity exercise. But they stayed segregated—because they weren't focused on the fact that they held the power to fix the situation.

The prof used this exercise to remind his students that they have convictions, but if they don't know them or speak up when they've been violated, they are wasting their voice. I am so proud of my girl for speaking up and attempting to point out the crazy. I pray that next time she'll hold on tighter. A little more like the character we see in Ruth from the Old Testament.

How Tightly Do You Cling?

Let's pick up this story in the first chapter of Ruth. Naomi has just lost her husband and both sons, and she's left living in a land far from home with two Moabite daughters-in-law. Although they have been family for about ten years, these girls were raised in a foreign culture with false gods. Naomi decides that, with all the hurt they've endured, it's time for her to head back to her hometown of Bethlehem. Both girls agree to join her. At first.

Somewhere along the trip, Naomi decides her widowed daughters have no future with her. They are better off returning to Moab to their own families. Orpah cries, but she agrees and turns back. Ruth, however, doesn't simply refuse to go; "Ruth clung to her" (Ruth 1:14 NIV).

This word "clung," translated from the Hebrew word *dabaq*, is the same word God uses when he says man and woman cleave to one another in marriage. To cling in this way is an inseparable covenant between two people—a perfect meld where we can no longer tell where one ends and the other begins because they are so aligned in their ways. Ruth sealed the deal by saying, "Don't urge me to leave you or to turn back from you. Where you go I will go, and where you stay I will stay. Your people will be my people and your God my God. Where you die I will die, and there I will be buried. May the LORD deal with me, be it ever so severely, if even death separates you and me" (Ruth 1:16–17 NIV). Even until death, Ruth refused to be separated from her mother-in-law. This is how I want my children to hold fast to their convictions.

When everyone else around them is saying and doing and being something else. I want my kids to stand up, even in the face of so-called authority, and say, "This isn't right. I won't continue. You will never part me from what I believe."

The End of Your Reach

There comes an age when your arms are suddenly shorter than they used to be. When you can no longer reach your son or daughter like you used to. Early on, you need to find yourself some synthetic arms. These are usually attached to other trusted parents in your community.

As our kids become teens and begin the final stretch of maturity, they naturally begin to pull away. That's as it should be. But it doesn't mean they should be left to do and be whomever or whatever. If we've been intentional early about surrounding our kids with healthy adults, our children won't see where our arms end and those of other adults begin. The transition is nearly seamless.

We are a village. These village people point our kids to prayer and respectful relationships. They hold our kids accountable to boundaries when we aren't around to see a breech. Most importantly, these village people redirect our children to God's face when the way gets hard. We can confidently hand our kids over to these safe relationships and trust that God is still writing their stories.

14

Your Kids' Testimony

*In your hearts revere Christ as Lord. Always be prepared to give
an answer to everyone who asks you to give the reason for the
hope that you have. But do this with gentleness and respect.*
—1 PETER 3:15 (NIV)

$\mathcal{G}$eorge Santayana once wrote, "Those who cannot remember the past are condemned to repeat it." And it is vital we learn the truths in this statement and teach them to our children. If we ignore the past and the lessons presented in the lives of so many Bible characters, we fail to learn from our mistakes. Instead we risk repeating them, and we miss the chance to pass along a biblical heritage that teaches our children to learn from our lives and from all of their ancestors. We and our children miss the valuable accomplishments in our biblical family history that help us to avoid the mistakes altogether.

Two Sides of the Same Coin

All of our history as a civilization is important, but let's narrow our history lesson down to biblical truths. On the one hand, parents, pastors, Sunday school teachers, aunties, and uncles need to guide our children to learn from others' mistakes. Teach them the mistakes of Peter; let them figure out what Judas Iscariot could have (and should have) done differently. Some of the stories we skim over in the Bible are saucy and uncomfortable, and yet they are a part of our history God intends us to know. If there was no value in their telling, the sometimes scandalous stories would not have made it into the pages of God's Word. The flip side of this coin is a little easier to take.

As we learn our own life lessons from Scripture, we must convey those lessons to our children. This happens as, page after amazing page, we focus on the willing men and women God used. Unfortunately, many children know just as little about the heroes of the Bible as they do the shady stories. Our kids need to have living examples to pull from when they are faced with a mighty giant, literally or figuratively. They need to *know* what Jesus would do, not just wear the bracelet. "Only be careful, and watch yourselves closely so that you do not forget the things your eyes have seen or let them fade from your heart as long as you live. Teach them to your children and to their children after them" (Deut. 4:9 NIV). The job is yours.

If I may repeat myself, I will repeat myself: *The job is yours.*

Let's begin with you. Do you know your testimony? When someone asks you—when your *kids* ask you—what you believe, why you believe it, where you came from, and where you are going, can you tell them? Will you stumble over your words or speak confidently as a sinner saved by grace? Will you speak in vague Christian lingo that leaves them confused and inferior because they don't know that language?

Maybe you have written your testimony before, so you feel like it is ready to go. But maybe you wrote it back in high school or just after you were married, so it's slightly outdated. If you know your testimony succinctly, you are ahead of the game. For the rest of us, let's take a minute and write it out.

Grab a fresh piece of lined paper or your prayer journal or a new Word document on your computer, and get going. Include where you were before you said yes to God, what made you finally say yes to God, and how you are different now that you have done so. Just a paragraph or two will do for most people. Do not overwhelm your story with details. Just lay it out.

When you are finished, if you feel your children can handle the scandal, share your story with your kids. Filter what you feel is too mature for them, but they need to know where they came from. They need to know who they are now because of it. They need to know where they are going. They need to know what they are up against. Your testimony is the perfect start to their journey.

Once you have your testimony intact, talk to your kids about their own stories. Share the Scripture from the beginning of this chapter out of 1 Peter: "In your hearts honor Christ the Lord as holy, always being prepared to make a defense to anyone who asks you for a reason for the hope that is in you; yet do it with gentleness and respect" (3:15 ESV). This Scripture is not instructing us to be defensive about our faith.

GI Joe thought he was just being clever, but truly, "Knowing is half the battle." It removes the surprise element and introduces the offense maneuvers to the game.

The Greek word used here for "defense" is *apologia*, the same word we use to get the English word *apologetics*.

This word is described as "the defense of the Christian faith." It alludes to the idea of offering an explanation for our faith. We need to share the proof of how God has moved in our lives. Changed us from a filthy sinner, not worthy to be in God's presence, to now standing in his overwhelming peace and forgiveness in a personal relationship. We need to share the experiences and thought processes that attended our acceptance of Christ, and the events that surrounded this transformation, so that others can understand our faith and God may be glorified for all of it.

To make a defense simply means to give a reason for the faith we have in Christ. To make a defense never means putting on our defendant pants and spouting our holiness for all to see (which would be lies anyway, right?). Nor does it mean berating our children with Scripture or with frightening tales of our past out of fear that their steps may follow too closely the footprints we have left behind. Fear should never motivate unless it is godly fear. In fact, 1 Peter 3:15 concludes with the mandate to use gentleness and respect. These attributes show themselves through our words.

Words Really Do Stick Like Glue

As much as we try to deny it, words spoken to us have the power to affect us for a lifetime. Ask adults about their favorite teacher and you will probably be inundated with smiles and happy stories about some great teacher who believed in their abilities. Conversely, ask an adult about a least-liked teacher and you will almost certainly hear about a teacher who said something awful that no human anywhere should say to anyone, especially a kid. Words are powerful. It is best we use them as God intended: as holy weapons.

> Middle schoolers have a special place in my heart. That's when I gave my life to God for the first time and dedicated my heart to Jesus and began having a relationship with him.
> —Randi, 20, Missionary kid

The writer of Hebrews says it this way: "For the word of God is alive and powerful. It is sharper than the sharpest two-edged sword, cutting between soul and spirit, between joint and marrow. It exposes our innermost thoughts and desires" (Heb. 4:12). This Scripture is saying that God's words, spoken to us from hundreds of years ago and now splashed across numerous translucent, white pages, have divine powers.

Do you believe it? This Scripture asks for no effort on our part to make it powerful. It requires nothing of our actions, our responses, or our circumstances to make these words great. God's words *are* powerful, and that is that. He does not need *us* or our power for his words to be mighty. However, to claim this mighty power for our lives and our children's lives, we must believe and *use* his words. How marvelous that we have been given something so powerful to stand on, or rather, fight with.

In his letter to the Ephesians, Paul says it another way:

> Put on every piece of God's armor so you will be able to resist the enemy in the time of evil. Then after the battle you will still be standing firm. Stand your ground, putting on the belt of truth and the body armor of God's righteousness. For shoes, put on the peace that comes from the Good News so that you will be fully prepared. In addition to all of these, hold up the shield of faith to stop the fiery arrows of the devil. Put on salvation as your helmet, and take the sword of the Spirit, which is the word of God. (6:13–17)

May I be so bold as to say that none of these come about simply by wanting them but by taking action and being intentional with our words and daily life choices.

The weapons Paul writes of are all gifts from God, but we have to accept them by faith and take action before they become game changers in our lives. We have been given God's ways (through the Bible) so we can exist in this world. His ways include walking forward in peace and truth, holding up faith like a shield (which includes being ready to make a defense), and effectively applying the Word of God. God has supplied our every need for protection, including body armor. His words are powerful all on their own. But for them to be lived out in us, we have to believe these words are meant for us and make a move!

Paul continues this passage of Scripture by admonishing us to speak incessantly, praying in the Spirit. We've all met that kid who won't stop talking, even when everyone has stopped listening. OK, maybe we shouldn't be so obnoxious, but the sentiment is the same. We are instructed to pray "at all times and on every occasion. Stay alert and be persistent in your prayers for all believers everywhere" (Eph. 6:18). How often does God want to hear from us? All the time. Running dialogue. At every interval.

In 2012, two things happened simultaneously that offer a picture of this verse. First my love for game shows, specifically *Wheel of Fortune*, meant my kids and I gathered around the television most nights for a little old-fashioned family TV time. I loved it. They loved it. Plus, they thought I was miraculous when I solved most of the puzzles.

Unfortunately, the second circumstance was not as happy. Hurricane Sandy left a devastating impression on the East Coast, and the reports of injury, death, and destruction rolled in for days. Every night brought an interruption of regularly scheduled programing to give an update, usually a sad one. We prayed and sought God's mercy for this situation and the families affected. It was no small happening. Lives were changing forever; family dynamics were being altered by displacement, loss of loved ones, and the destruction of homes and businesses.

As my family gathered around the living room to out-Wheel each other, I noticed the running ticker of news information across the bottom of the screen. One instant we were shouting out letters of suggestion, and the next my eyes were drawn to the scrolling updates. The ticker paused and I was back to the game.

I know what you are thinking—they are children. She will let them win. Not so much. This isn't Candy Land, people. When you stand in front of the Wheel, it's game on! (Grunt.)

These updates were relentless, mostly just saying the same thing or rewording old information. It didn't matter if the information was happy or sad. That little black strip was pervasive enough that it won my attention every time. Every two minutes. Even when I knew it simply repeated the same old thing.

God wants us to be that running tape of news information. He wants us to come to him in praise, in thanksgiving, with hurts, when we need help, when we need direction, and when we want to celebrate breakthroughs. He wants full access to our ticker tape of information. Even if we feel it's the same old news.

Paul wraps up this portion of Scripture by asking for help. He knows that words, besides being his own weapon, can also be wielded by other believers to defend him and keep him on the path that sustains him. Look closely at Ephesians 6:18–20, and notice its key words and repeated requests. Paul pleads with believers to use their words to make *his* words clear to unbelievers.

> Pray in the Spirit at all times and on every occasion. Stay alert and be persistent in your prayers for all believers everywhere. And pray for me, too. Ask God to give me the right words so I can boldly explain God's mysterious plan that the Good News is for Jews and Gentiles alike. I am in chains now, still preaching the message as God's ambassador. So pray that I will keep on speaking boldly for him, as I should.

In a mere three sentences, Paul mentions different ways of communicating with words ten times: pray/prayers (four), right words, explain, Good News, preaching, message, and speaking. He was asking the Ephesians to side with him and fight so everyone, Jew and Gentile, would be open and willing to hear everything God wanted to say through him. In spite of being imprisoned, Paul was using his words as a weapon to fight for the salvation of those not yet following Christ. Everything was taken from Paul, yet this one weapon remained. Would you agree that Paul made a difference for the kingdom of God? He was a warrior.

In the same way that we would never send a soldier out to the front lines without protection and at least one weapon, we should take heart not to send our children forward without the same precautions. Their protection is prayer and faith. Their weapon is the Word of God and every promise within it. Our role as parents is to pray over them and train them to wear their armor and hold their sword of truth firmly.

The Bible Tells Us So

The best family activity you may ever do over the course of your child's life is memorize Scriptures together. And not just any Scripture. Sit with your children and find Scriptures that encourage them through their own real-life situations. Target Scriptures that align with their own testimonies. This is not a time for ambiguity.

Look for specifics in Scripture that match your child's life. Are you a family that moves often for work or financial reasons? Study Abraham or Moses. These men learned that home was where God led them and everywhere they went along the way. Is your child suffering from seemingly endless fears? Cling to the Psalms that talk about God's protection, or memorize the story of Joshua and what he was able to accomplish in the face of fear. Joshua spoke three very small words to a mighty God and was seemingly nonchalant about their outcome: "Sun, stand still" (Josh. 10:12 NIV).

Does your child feel like the only kid at her high school who chooses to be a Christian, even throughout the week when friends are looking? Give her Esther's words to lean on. Her cousin Mordecai directed her to be bold and speak up for those who couldn't defend themselves. He said, "Who knows but that you have come to your royal position for such a time as this?" (Esther 4:14 NIV). After some encouragement, prayer, and fasting, Esther sent Mordecai a message: "I will go to the king, even though it is against the law. And if I perish, I perish" (v. 16 NIV).

Esther and Mordecai both knew what he meant by the question "Who knows . . . ?" He meant, "God knows. Be encouraged. Take heart, and take God with you. But no matter what you do, *move*! Do not sit in fear; rather, be strong and courageous."

We do not have to make up encouraging words to help our children stand strong. God promises that he is "a shield around me" (Ps. 3:3). Let his Word take over your family's vernacular, and just see what a difference it makes in your children.

Aptly Named

In keeping with this look at history—at our biblical ancestors, our personal pasts, and our children's beginnings—now is a good time to share with your child the meaning behind his or her name. Now, before you go find that stash of rotting cabbage again, let me acknowledge that not every one of our children will have a meaningful name. I know this. I have these kids. It's just that *if* your child was named after a relative or some amazing person, or if their name has some particular significance, they should know.

We spend *so* much time deliberating over what to name a kid, and then we fail to share the story. Let's fix that. And don't just tell a child once. We all know the best tactic for remembering anything is repetition. My children love to hear how we came up with their names. Just like those little birdies in the egg, they love that we spent so much time and energy preparing for their arrival.

Our names can (and should) define us. Esther means "star," as in a small light in a dark time. Samuel means "God has heard." How encouraged will my son Sam be to know God hears him? David means "beloved." Every time a mama calls her little man by that name, she is calling him beloved. How loved will this kid feel if he knows this from early on? I was delighted to learn that my own name means "song." I would say my name defines me completely as I am always singing, and it's one of my favorite gifts from God.

I was less thrilled to learn my dad got my name from an old Sandra Dee movie. He only passed it on to me because his parents wouldn't let him name the poodle Shontell. That's just fine. Fine. Thanks, Dad.

131

See What God Sees

You do not know the future God has for your children. God knows, which is why he has called you to govern your babies to follow after him. He has great plans for your children.

Jesse (1 Samuel 16) was the father of a great many boys. The prophet, Samuel, came to Jesse's house in obedience to God's directions to go to Bethlehem: "I have chosen one of his sons to be king" (v. 1 NIV). Seven boys paraded in front of Samuel hoping to be the chosen son. I picture each dressed up in his fiercest gear to look the part. No doubt Jesse was #goals proud of his big, strapping boys. The Bible suggests they were pleasant in appearance and of a height to intimidate in war.

Samuel looked and considered the sons one at a time, but each of Jesse's boys was passed over. "Are these all the sons you have?" Samuel asked (v. 11).

Jesse admitted that one lowly boy was not present. Lowly because he was the youngest, coming out of his gawky early-teen years, and his job was that of a mere servant: tend the sheep. Samuel had his orders, and he held fewer preconceived notions about the way God chooses people. He insisted everyone in the room remain standing until David was fetched from the field. Then the Lord spoke: "Anoint him" (v. 12).

So Samuel did. David was anointed as king with oil by one of the greatest prophets, sent by God, in front of his brothers (who were #ungoals passed over) and his father (who brushed off the potential that God saw in his boy).

Who Are You Most Like?

Put yourself in everyone's shoes. Whose fit you best?

Are you David because people ignore your potential? Are you one of the brothers, looking down on those God calls because you are jealous that your hard work and good looks have not landed you a God-appointed position in leadership or among your friends or at church? Are you Jesse, deciding who is good enough to help God? Are you

Samuel, disregarding the world's view of a person and seeing what God sees in him or her?

Who are you? And how does that affect your child? Your son has amazing potential. Your daughter has a God-designed path. Your kids have the capability to take down a giant or start a trend of vulnerable, laid-bare worship, and they have the goods to lead nations. Your son or daughter has what it takes to be a modern-day David. They need you to be their Samuel, believing in them and focusing on the potential God has placed within them.

15

Partners in Crime

Giorraíonn beirt bóthar. (Two shorten the road.)
—IRISH PROVERB

$\mathcal{I}$ realize not all our Missionary Mamas are married, but you may have been at one point, or possibly will be sometime in the future, so this chapter is worth the read for everyone. Also, biological dads are not the only father figures you might interact with as you raise your babies. This chapter is about those other men too.

I hope you are beginning to appreciate the hefty amount of fighting tools we are given in this game of raising kids. Our words, *the* Word, God's promises, and a healthy dose of proactivity mixed with intentionality set us firmly on a foundation only God could orchestrate. But there is another key element to parenting that often gets sabotaged before we realize it's happening. One of your best defenses is a solid relationship with your spouse.

Your Marriage Matters

As deeply as we've studied our armor and weapons, we also have to make ourselves aware of the devil's grand scheme. Our vile enemy comes to destroy the family dynamic of a happy marriage at the forefront. His mission is to make us believe God's plan for marriage and family will not work. He mixes up our purpose of marriage and throws a smoke screen over our priorities until they are messed up just enough that they still seem honorable.

Let me ask a (hopefully) silly question. Who among you, when asked why you were getting married, ever said, "So I can have kids"? I am fairly confident none of you raised your hand just now. Why then do we so easily fall into the routine of pushing our spouses so far onto the back burner that we forget everything about them until our kids move out of the house? We do the same thing to ourselves, putting the kids at the top of the pyramid.

By the time the kids are gone, husband and wife are so far removed from one another they have no recollection of what brought them together in the first place. Ah, the devil's subtle ways! This one happens before we realize it and usually leaves couples feeling as if it's too late to fix their relationship.

I have watched this heartbreaking scenario play out in too many marriages to call it unusual. The pattern is a wily conspiracy the devil dreamed up to move us further from God's plan, grace, and protection and into the scary land of self-justification (aka sin). If satan can get even one of the spouses to believe everything they do is for the children, he wins a battle.

Our enemy is not a brilliant cat, yet he gets us feuding *every* Sunday before church. He's the loser in this game, but we keep letting him in for a few plays here and there. That's all he is asking for, because he knows it's all he needs. In the span of ten seconds—just enough to break eye contact with our heavenly Father—suddenly we've introduced space not only between us and God but also between husband and wife. And because kids have what always feel like immediate needs, we are off chasing their needs down a rabbit hole, leaving our spouse in the dust. What's wrong with doing things for our kids anyway, right?

And they are loud. Oh so loud.

Don't satan's schemes sound so obvious? We think, "satan could never trick me so easily." When it's written in black and white, it's blatant. But the enemy doesn't function out there in the apparent. We would see right through him. He lingers in the subtleties. How many times have you heard a friend, coworker, fellow church member, or complete stranger say one of the following:

- We don't have sex much anymore. The two-year-old simply won't sleep unless I hold her all night long.
- We don't really have the money, but I don't want my kids to go without like I had to. I want them to have everything.
- We are staying married for the kids.

These out-of-whack priorities reek of the serpent in the garden. Mostly truth. They're just one step to the left of real, where half the time we still have our eyes on the parts that look good, so it seems like we are still in the right place. We aren't bothering to look down to see where we are standing. If we did, we would see we've been lured away from God's truths. We would see we are leaning into sketchy shadows instead of standing firmly in God's light. The problem here is that we cannot properly raise our children to be lights in this world if we do not take care of our marriages first and foremost, because shadows do not beget light.

Many of us have these half-truths we've put on like cloaks. We believe they are simply a part of our lives now. Take a minute and ask God to reveal yours. Then untie it and toss it.

This habit of off-kilter priorities may take a little while to correct, but it's fixable. Being a wife is a major role, one full of blessing in a way no other relationship can offer. To be so at one with another person—cleaved to him—is second only to our relationship with Jesus Christ himself. Other than true redemption with our Savior, being one with our spouse is one of the greatest presents God gives us in our earthly lives.

I know this is big. Being a wife *and* a Missionary Mom carries weight. I cannot offer you a cure-all formula to make your worries disappear or make this load lighter. But I can help you decide which priorities you want at the forefront. We can weed through others you are willing to let go of, even if you are only setting them down for a little while. This intentional action creates space in your everyday so that Hubby lands in his rightful spot.

This is the soul-searching part of the book where we get real with how we are living and allow God to speak up in the areas where we might be missing the mark. We put forth the question to our husbands and God: "Are we growing together each day to become who God intends us to be?" That little phrase, "become who God intends," is what we will focus on next.

Your Road to Becoming

"Who God intends us to be"—*what* does that mean? First let's look at who we are. This is the best way to see who we are teaching our children to become. Because I don't actually know you, I will volunteer to be the example and share who I want to be when I grow up.

Yet . . . I don't know you yet. I dream big.

Foremost, I am a Christian. *After* that, God has made me a wife, mother, daughter, sister, and friend. In these roles I have certain duties and responsibilities that I must do if I want to avoid the consequences that follow from my more lazy or rebellious side. It's basic cause and effect. If I don't keep my kitchen floor clean, I will likely be the one to find the jelly spill on my freshly donned socks, right? I will probably yell

For the record, this is the order I believe our priorities fall in as lived out in our daily lives. Many women struggle to put their husband before the kids, but trust me, ladies, this is exactly how God meant it. (See 1 Peter 3.)

No One In Particular is the guy I talk to when no one else listens. "Who are you talking to, dear?" "Oh, No One In Particular." We talk often.

at No One In Particular, and because of the yelling, I won't notice the full impact the jelly is having on my life until I notice the sticky tracks leading halfway up my carpeted stairs. Translation: Lazy bones equal sticky stairs and a Grumpy Gus disposition.

Far-fetched? Maybe, but this happens too often in my house, and I always seem to be in fresh socks. As the wife of a man who truly feels loved when he sees a well-cared-for home, I am called to clean that home. Or at least to delegate that chore so it gets done well.

He receives love through acts of service. Why, God? Why!

I am also called to honor my husband, respect him with my actions and words, and love him more than I love myself. This is a huge order for a girl who was born the baby and only girl in a family of four kids. *What?* It's not like I asked for the attention—at first. I will ever be a work in progress, but the point is that I am working toward what God calls righteous. Here's where I tell you a story about how not to partner with your spouse and raise kids.

The Saddest Conjunction in the Bible

The story of how God connects Isaac and Rebekah is miraculous. Straight out of a Hollywood-type screenplay full of miracles, scandal, and suspense. Mid Genesis takes us down the path of Isaac's life from his miraculous conception to the salvation scene on the mountain, and from his God-ordained engagement to his wife Rebekah's miraculous conception after twenty years of barrenness. A true Genesis drama.

Rebekah delivers twin boys after a tumultuous pregnancy. Although the twins share a birthday, the firstborn, Esau, holds the rights to best blessings and best inheritance. He is heir to everything. But in an overly dramatic performance of "I can't possibly go another second without food, so much so that I will promise you anything if you feed me," Esau promises his younger-by-minutes brother his birthright. Things continue to get worse from there, and I can pretty much pinpoint the source of the problems: "Isaac loved Esau because he enjoyed eating the wild game Esau brought home, but Rebekah loved Jacob" (Gen. 25:28).

But. *But?* What in the world is this sentence telling us? That each parent played favorites? That Isaac had much in common with Esau, so it was easier to love him? That Rebekah needed Jacob to feel loved as well, so she overcompensated and maybe even resented Esau a little bit? Can you function as a mother this way, loving one child more than another? This one word "but" is where the story completely derails. Oh, but it gets better.

> **God has given me an amazing spouse who is different than I am but similar to the parts of my children I don't understand.**
> **—Melissa, Missionary Mom of two**

In chapter 27, Rebekah moves from overprotective, dicey mother to accomplice. Isaac asks his son Esau to hunt and prepare some food. He's setting up for something close to his final meal as he is nearing death, and he wants to bestow his eldest with the blessing due his firstborn miracle. Rebekah overhears this plan and devises her own maniacal scheme for Jacob. She goes so far as to cover Jacob in goatskin so Isaac, nearly blind with age, will think he is talking to Esau (who happens to be significantly hairy). And it works. Jacob brings in goat stew and pretends to be Isaac's favorite. He receives Esau's blessing. It appears that Jacob pulls the rug right out from under his brother and his father—but it's both parents who are left holding the rug . . . red-handed.

Somewhere along the way, Rebekah lost sight of her role as Missionary Mom. She allowed one tiny word—*but*—to change her course and launch her twin baby boys into decades of feuding and turmoil. God laid an opportunity at her feet to raise up nations, but her focus was all wrong. Her priorities were not rooted in raising Missionary kids. And her family suffered for decades.

A Final Word

Families may have one parent whose priorities are way out of whack. Sometimes the destruction devolves into fully absent parents and even parents in jail. Broken homes seem more prevalent than ever, with moms and dads going it alone or from separate houses. I won't pretend these are easy obstacles, but God cares too much about you and your children to leave you alone.

If you have an absent dad in your raising-kids game, find a new one. I am not talking about remarrying or finding a relationship for yourself. I mean, go look for good, solid, godly men who are willing to step up where someone else isn't. Maybe there are such men in your extended family, or go to church, speak to youth leaders, even set up an old-fashioned family night with your kids and these father figures so your kids have a steady role model of what it means to be a trustworthy man. Ask God to put godly men in your kids' lives. He loves to hand-deliver miracles like that.

Family dynamics are as varied as flavors of ice cream. No two families are the same, even those that, at a glance, seem similar. But one thing is true across the board: you simply can't raise that baby alone. So use what you've got to work with, and then go find other people to fill in the gaps.

16

Parenting on Purpose: I Meant to Do That

Obey your father's commands,
and don't neglect your mother's instruction.
Keep their words always in your heart.
Tie them around your neck.
When you walk, their counsel will lead you.
When you sleep, they will protect you.
When you wake up, they will advise you.
—PROVERBS 6:20–22

*M*y husband walked into the living room the other day and flashed me his belly button. "Look!" he exclaimed.

Having no idea why I was chosen to take part in his navel display, I offered a supportive, "Cool. You have a belly button. Me too!" I proceeded to show him mine.

I know this seems weird. And it was, especially considering our children were all sitting in the living room witnessing this exchange. The disgust on their faces was priceless! I was cracking up—and I was still totally lost as to what my husband was trying to convey.

Turns out he was pointing to the button on his pants. A button he had asked me to sew on at least two years ago. He loved *OK, four.* these pants so much that he wore them even without the button. *For four years.* About three times a month, he would hold them up and say wistfully, "Man, I love these pants," or, "I sure wish someone would sew this button back onto my favorite pants. They are my most favoritest pants in the whole wide world." He would look off into the distance forlornly. And because he is from Indiana, he would suddenly get his accent back.

It's as if he was transported to another time and his name was Opie and his dad's name was Andy. (Classic case of laying it on thick.)

From the corner of my eye, I saw my sixteen-year-old son beaming. My husband clarified: "I should have just asked Elijah to sew this button on all those years ago. He did it in about five minutes. He even had his own needle and thread."

"Oh, good," I said. "I taught him how to sew ages ago. So it's as if I too sewed this button on for you. You're very welcome." After *Alone.* laughing hysterically, I gave Eli all the credit. I was very proud of that kid. It got me thinking about how many times I have intentionally taught my children life skills—and wondering how many teachable moments I had missed.

So I made a list. A physical one.

To Do Today (and Tomorrow)

I think you should make a list too. It doesn't matter how old your kids are. They could be six days from their eighteenth birthday or about to celebrate their first steps as a bitty baby. As a Missionary Mom, you have the chance to think ahead to the kind of kid you want rolling out in society with your last name. You are intentionally giving them instructions to tie about their necks. These are some of the things Proverbs 6:21 is talking about.

Begin jotting. Use the margins of this book, use Post-it Notes, but whatever you use, make

"My son, keep your father's command and do not forsake your mother's teaching. Bind them always on your heart; fasten them around your neck" (Prov. 6:20–21 NIV).

142

it something that will last, so you can keep referring to it over the span of whatever time you've got left. If we start from the get-go, we have eighteen Christmases to squeeze in everything. I know it sounds a little early to teach life skills to a one-year-old, but how many of you taught your baby to wave when someone said hello? Aren't you teaching your child to greet someone properly? It isn't just a wave. It's the jumping-off point to manners when speaking to others.

Last week I taught nineteen kindergartners to shake hands and greet one another with their name and eye contact. For some of them, this was a breeze. Others were reduced to fits of uncomfortable giggles. We had fun with it, but it was clear which students have a proactive mom at home making the most of even the small opportunities. There's an intentionality that comes when we move from Mom to Missionary.

Here are some things I hope to teach each of my kiddos before they move out. These are in no order, and there always seems to be something new to add to the list.

Life Skills To-Do List

Shake hands and meet new people

Sew on a button and make simple seams

Make a good pot of coffee

Cook at least two food items for each meal

Properly clean a bathroom

Roll a sleeping bag

Know how and what to recycle

Donate items to a thrift store

Pump gas

Sweep and mop a floor

Change the oil in their car, or at least find the right person to do so

Change a tire

Read the warning dials on their vehicle

Make an appointment with a doctor, dentist, or other service provider

Have a proper phone conversation

Do laundry—all of it, including ironing and dry cleaning

Manage money, including building a savings and tithing

Use social media responsibly

Get a job

Keep a job

Quit a job

Have quiet time with God

Keep a file of important information

File taxes

Know what to do in an emergency

Be a good roommate

Pray

Confront a brother or sister in Christ

Create a menu plan

Host a guest in their home

Load a dishwasher efficiently

Travel in a group

Rent an apartment, car, paddleboard, etc.

Paint a room

Use common household tools

Stay in touch with others (especially their mama) when things get busy or stressful

Haggle—know when and how to haggle well, and know when the seller needs the money more than we need to save a buck

Use an ATM

Lose well

Win better

Bring a meal to someone struggling or sick

Write and send thank-you notes

Know how to use snail mail

Dress for the occasion

Realize that decisions are temporary, not forever, unless it's a tattoo (so you better pray long and hard over that decision)

Learn basic self-defense

I know the prospect of a list can feel a little overwhelming, especially if you are reading this book in your baby's senior year in high school. But creating a list puts actions to our parenting. I am constantly thinking of how I can turn a situation into a learning experience. Because these thoughts are already tucked away in my brain (or written on a sheet of paper in my Bible), I'm quick to see a learning situation and put my kids in the middle of it so they get the experience. You can too. Whether you have six hundred days left or just six before Junior moves out, you can pick and implement action steps that are vital and attainable in that time frame.

> Take road trips with your kids. The best possible conversations happen when you strip away all the outside distractions and it's just you two in the car. —Jessica, Missionary Mom of three

Being a Missionary Mom isn't only about imparting our spiritual understanding. The role of a missionary is to pass along our knowledge so effectively that those we minister to are able to turn around and continue passing it along. With these skills, our children become successful humans out in the world from a young age. All of these practical steps matter almost as much as the spiritual side. These abilities make our children more capable missionaries.

That Awkward Moment

Practical application and spiritual life are two vital areas where we want to be proactive as parents. One category we can't forget is tackling the moral dilemmas.

Plenty of times I wait for an opportunity to pop up to raise the sticky questions. When my boy was in middle school, we ran some errands. We chatted about whatever, and then I asked a real humdinger: "What would you do if a kid at school showed you a pornographic magazine?"

I tossed it out like it was everyday conversation and as if my guts weren't all a jumble, because I want my son to feel like talking with his mom about big issues is everyday. Heavy topics between mom and son are normal. Easy.

His face was all, "Aaugh!" and Charlie Brown, but he played it cool. He even spent a few minutes being thoughtful (or pretending he was someplace happy and far, far away) and said, "I would say, 'I don't want to see that.'"

I conveyed that I was proud of him and encouraged him to take it a little further if he felt brave enough. We talked about how he could encourage his friend to stop looking as well. He decided he could talk to other kids that might be tempted to look and set the example of opting out. Nothing big would need to be said, just a simple "No, thanks. That girl's daddy would not appreciate us looking at her that way."

The best part of our conversation came after I thought we had wrapped it up. About five minutes later, he threw out, "Why did you ask me that question?"

"Because I love you, and I don't want you to have to decide what you'll do after you've been faced with that situation. You'll be much smarter in your response if you've got a plan going in. Looking at pictures or videos like that can be tempting, but it's also addicting. And once you see it, it seems to stick in your mind like a stain. I don't want that for you."

After another couple minutes of quiet, he tacked on, "Thanks, Mama. That's a good idea. Pretty awkward, but a good idea." We both laughed out loud. So add "awkward conversations" to your list as well.

Adulting

At the time of writing this, I have only had a real adult child for a little over a year. Admittedly my experience in this is limited, but I have enough traction in the game to know she is still learning from me. Since she's moved out, we've navigated talking to her tuition office, interacting with an awkward roommate, and knowing when to notify school police because she is beginning to believe she has a stalker.

Yes, a real-life, overstepping-boundaries, inappropriate-interactions stalker. In this last case, she learned that sometimes her mama will handle the entire situation. Her mama and the police. She still gets to be protected. In other issues we encourage her to stand on her own.

Not all the items on your list may be appropriate for your family or necessary to teach. Some may be just a matter of prayer. And you may find that your kids teach themselves—some of them through trial and error. You can be systematic with your list or just keep it handy and choose a few that are right for your season of parenting.

Some of the skills will be quick and light; others will be heavy and may even reveal some things in our children that aren't shining qualities. Don't take it personally. When our kids sin, it isn't automatically a reflection on our parenting. It's a reflection of satan's hand on earth. We know we are sinners—all of us. It does no good spending time asking why our kids behave the way they do. We know why. Instead, we get to spend our time thinking of ways to combat our naturally inborn sin nature by proactively parenting our children.

Don't ask your kids either. No good comes of it. We know why.

17

Loving Others: Stateside Missions

As you come to him, the living Stone—rejected
by humans but chosen by God and precious to
him—you also, like living stones,
are being built into a spiritual house.
—1 PETER 2:4–5 (NIV)

My son and daughter go to the oldest high school in the city. It's steeped in traditions dating back one hundred years, and many of the teachers working there attended as students themselves. We've only been in this neighborhood for about three years, but even as newbies, my kids feel part of something much larger because of the culture and love for community. One teacher in particular adds much of this tradition. Her name is Newbs.

Newbs

Actually, her name is Amie Newberry, but to her students that's too formal. They have fully bought in to her approach in teaching them, which makes her come across as everyone's favorite auntie rather than a teacher. Heck, every time I run into her I want her to be *my* auntie too! How does she achieve this? I am sure it can't be pinned to one thing, but she does something that resembles a Missionary Mom move.

She requires the students in her advanced-placement English classes to volunteer and serve the community for ten hours each school year. Two or three times a year she coordinates some outing where these kids serve dinner to the elderly, box up meals at the local food pantry, or conduct some other small act of kindness.

For many of these kids, this will be the first and maybe the only time they'll participate in something that cares for someone else. For others, it will be just another way to give something back, even if they are only doing it for a grade. And some kids will say this is a typical Saturday; they do this sort of thing all the time. No matter what their experience, Newbs's expectations make them a team focused on others more than themselves, even if it's just for a few hours on a Saturday.

She's sending the message that they are part of something bigger, and they have the opportunity to be a light to others. What she's done is point out their own hands and feet and given them a voice to go along with it all. More importantly, she's helped teach these kids that loving a community is easy and fun and fulfilling. She's Missionary Mommed them right in the middle of a public school English class.

I think this setup works so well because of her approach. She doesn't send the kids home with a letter asking them to find a way to help someone in the community. There are no assignments asking students to write about how great people in history served others. She pulls them under her wing and says, "Let's go. Let's be all-in together." And then she brings them along with her to serve. This is the exact model we can follow as we teach our kids to love well right inside their communities.

Teach Them to Serve

Think back to those mama birds speaking to their babies through their eggshells at the start of this book. Think about those baby puppies mimicking their mama in her crawling. Not once did either of those mothers send their kiddos out and merely hope for the best. They led the way, and they did so in pretty close proximity. This example of serving well can start when our kids are still itty bitties.

Five-year-olds can serve. Six-year-olds can clean up after themselves at a restaurant. Ten-year-olds can pull the neighbor's weeds just because it's a Thursday and it needs to be done. Fifteen-year-olds can cook, clean, and host Taco Tuesday for their communities. And the whole time, we get to stand right there serving alongside them in either our city or our church.

Tacos: It's What Jesus Would Do

When my children became tweens, we began to realize they were spending more time with other kids and families that we didn't know very well. We did the meet-and-greet before dropping them off for a play date or hangout or whatever it's called when you're in middle school. But that left us with superficial information and standing outside of our children's relationships. Even if we chose to have that other kiddo over to our house, it left me feeling as if the connection between families was segregated. As much as my twelve-year-old at the time thought she was totally ready to navigate the relationships in her life, I knew she wasn't really ready to be without us.

> I contribute a sense of "togetherness" in our home. Wow, that sounds totally corny, but I'm usually the one that will initiate "family time" or come up with ideas for our family to have fun together. —Laura, Missionary Mom of two

My brother used to host dinner at his house and let his kids invite people to come over to get to know them a little more. He and his wife served everyone tacos and placed themselves back in the mix. It was just what we needed to keep our kids within reach while allowing them to attempt new relationships with those outside our immediate circle.

When we started our own Taco Tuesday, we stepped in with a few goals in mind. My husband and I wanted to know any person who claimed to be part of our children's lives. This included coaches, teachers, kids, classmates, neighbors, mentors, youth leaders, teammates, and even potential dates. In addition to knowing these people, we wanted them to get to know us. To put faces to our names and know just a little bit more of our take on what we expect of our children when they are away from us.

Taco Tuesday was an instant hit. I can't *You had me at* even remember how many years we have been *tacos. It wouldn't* hosting it, but we've learned a couple things. *matter if you* After trying things this way and that and *were asking me to* tweaking our way through a few dinners, we *trade my oldest* realized that hosting once a month is right for *child. If it involves* our family. More than that gets in the way *guacamole, I'm* of my mellow weeknight vibe, and it costs a *weak.* little more than I want to spend on groceries.

We also realized that we don't have to foot the bill for much. Some kids offer to bring something for the tacos, but usually we add this to the list of things we teach our guests. It's polite to ask, "What can I bring?" when you're invited to a meal. If they don't offer, I ask. Feeling awkward yet? Don't! As it turns out, teenagers love having a purpose. Even more than showing up for a free dinner and hangout, they love bringing a diced onion. I had a kid bring diced tomatoes one night. I'll be honest. When I asked her to bring tomatoes I didn't expect so much conversation about the whole thing that night.

"Here! I brought the tomatoes. Sorry it's so many. This is probably way too much, but I've never diced a tomato before, and I loved it! So I just kept dicing. I had to watch a video online to learn how to do it. I feel so accomplished!"

This wasn't a one-time conversation. She brought it up about three times to different people, and I swear her face was full of joy. Over tomatoes. Tomatoes and being part of something bigger than her typical face glued to a screen or self-serving ways we are so used to in a world of human nature. I didn't ask her to join me for an African mission trip where we fed three hundred children working in a mine. At no time were we handing out tracts to the homeless. Nope. I asked her to bring tomatoes and join us for dinner in my backyard.

The only thing that rivals interacting with my children's community of people is the debrief that happens after they leave. The family ends most nights gathered in our squashed living room on an oddly padded old couch. All of us just migrate there, and we chat about everything and nothing and anything ridiculous that needs telling. We laugh, we argue sometimes, and we nearly always pray before bed. It's just our routine. On Taco Tuesdays, our conversation often settles around what *my* kids learned about other families.

"You know what's weird," one of them will usually start off. "Jace kept saying, 'Man, this is so weird. You eat dinner with your parents?'" Or someone will casually throw out, "My friends think it's really weird that we like each other. They said they only fight with their siblings, or they stay in their rooms all the time and never talk." As we settle into our nighttime routine of prayers and kisses, we get to explain what's different and the choices we make to be an intentionally loving family.

Sometimes the things these other kiddos notice brings me to tears because no one should be confused as to why I am excited to see my husband when he comes home from work. It shouldn't be foreign to a wife that a husband is helping with dinner or setting up chairs in the backyard for a get-together. Laughter shouldn't be seldom in a house. And the bad days should never outweigh the good days. If this is the case, then we aren't leading our families well. If this is true, then we aren't leading our Christian homes any differently than everyone else.

It Doesn't Have to Be Tacos

I don't even know when I began loving tacos so much. Possibly my love-love relationship with tacos began in high school during my first date with my now husband, Handsome. I ran through *#tacosaremyjam*

Taco Bell's drive-through and purchased ten hard-shell tacos and a small Dr. Pepper to fill the gaping hole in my belly left from four hours of volleyball conditioning and not nearly enough food. With thirty minutes to shower and change before Handsome showed up, I ate all ten of those tacos like a Hoover devours a baby sock. Gone before I knew what was happening.

Ten tacos. This is not an exaggeration.

We went on our date—a steamy hour of researching over microfiche at the library. He invited me to grab a bite to eat on our way home. Lost in those dreamy blue eyes, I said yes before I knew what I was agreeing to. Because (A) those ten tacos were still smack-dab in the center of my stomach, (2) I had four dollars to my name, and (d) one hour is not nearly enough time to warrant more food. So we went to Applebee's, and I ordered a small side salad with my four bucks and overly full stomach. Immediately he side-glanced me and mumbled his disappointment. "You aren't one of those girls who just eats salad, are you?"

Oh, the shame! I almost couldn't make eye contact with that guy as I said, "I ate ten tacos right before you picked me up." I am pretty sure he knew he wanted to marry me in that exact minute. Plus, he paid for my salad. It was an evening of winning and the start to something oh so beautiful. For your family, it could be something totally different than tacos.

If Not Tacos, Then What?

Think back to all those things you love to do that revive your brain. Pick one of those and make it a monthly staple for your family where your kids invite their people. Volleyball at the marina, soccer in the park, a potluck at your house, or anything whatsoever that creates space for other families to come and feel loved. A place where tweens, teens, coaches, teachers, and whoever else in your kid's village can come and know you and be known in return. Keep it basic.

Let the focus be on relationships, not on entertaining people. And most of all, be ready. Because when you make a bold move like this, God will begin to deliver people to your doorstep. Your family will start looking at your household just a little bit differently. Maybe even with a tad more appreciation for how well you love, even if it's loving them enough to say "No" or "Don't go" or "Not right now." And maybe you will get to rock some sixteen-year-old's world because you asked her to bring some tomatoes. Diced.

18

Am I Too Late?

This is the LORD's battle.
—1 SAMUEL 17:47

$\mathscr{T}$here are bound to be some of you reading this who say, "Sure. This is a novel idea, but my kid is already (fill in the blank age). I am too late." That's not quite accurate. I realize I have spent an entire book's worth of pages convincing you that you make a major difference in your child's life. I've bordered along the fine line between passion and broken record when I ask you to be intentional and proactive as a parent.

I am also a realist with firmly rooted feet. I know we all have different homes, children, relationships with other moms, relationships with God, and even very different husbands. Our backgrounds are radically different, and the people in our village are as different as Mars and Venus. This means how we've parented our children is going to be extremely different from house to house. It doesn't matter. What matters is that God is the writer of your child's story just as much as he is the author of yours. And he delights in both of you. He says you are capable and worth his time.

How David Did It

David's life was slightly cray. Roller coaster is an understatement for this guy. He fights giants with more confidence than I've seen in the most self-assured teenager. Ever. But then he turns and runs on repeat for a huge section of Scripture. Faith oozes from him one minute, and then the next he's hiding in a cave as King Saul takes a potty break. David's life plays like those movie moments where you are so pumped for the main character, and then you have to cover your eyes because the scene is too embarrassing to even look at it through finger cracks. They are totally blowing it.

Here's the thing about David. He was raised by a dad who didn't even count him as son enough to call him in from the field when a prophet came to meet his children. His dad, Jesse, gathered all his sons when he heard *He was apparently using air quotes around "all."* Samuel was in town. The boys purified them- selves and went to a good ole-fashioned animal sacrifice before anyone noticed David wasn't even in the room.

But here's the thing about *Samuel*. He realized obeying God was his most important job. And whether or not he knew it, choosing David was perhaps the most life-altering thing he would ever do. Samuel felt so strongly about waiting for David to come in from the field that he wouldn't let anyone sit down to eat until David showed up. Every time I imagine it, there's just a lot of awkward. Samuel was fine with that too, because his history with God gave him a whole lot of promises to stand on. Anointing David to the throne was about to create the lineage of Christ.

So whether your kid is six or sixteen, you have the chance to start now. Be willing to put a hold on dinner if that's what it comes to. Cancel your entire lives and declare a family-dynamic reset, banking on the fact that God calls your child beloved. Capable. Worth the investment.

Think Possibilities, Not Missed Opportunities
Your son or daughter is a thread in a grand tapestry of God's design. You get to put your kid in the game so he or she fulfills their calling.

Admittedly, starting this will not be as smooth as starting when they're young. But God is mighty. And he wants this to work. He also promises us that "This is the LORD's battle" (1 Sam. 17:47). Your kiddo may face a Goliath through this process, but everyone knows that Goliath falls. Hard. And David doesn't just win a little bit. He stands over Goliath's unconscious body and cuts off his head.

What's more, no one around David thought he could do it. When he faced Goliath, and later when he faced Saul, and even much later when David was king, he was surrounded by doubters. His own brothers turned on him first (1 Sam. 17:28)—a trait they learned from their father, no doubt, when Samuel first visited to see his sons (16:5–11). But God knew differently. And God knows differently for us too, because he looks upon our story as it should be, not in our limited, linear view of what seems to be unfolding.

God sees something in our kids that we hardly ever do. God sees how he is going to turn all the mess back around to his glory. He knows what's possible. We get to jump on board for what he has planned all along; we just have to decide this is so important that we will no longer let anything get in the way. Like Samuel putting a hold on dinner, we get to say, "Nothing else is as important as getting us back to the path God is laying out before us." And then do it.

Apology Accepted

Eons ago, my mom had four crazy little Afro-haired babies running amok in her kitchen. I was the youngest and only girl. There were three older brothers, all close in age and none wilder than the youngest, Shane. With four kids under the age of seven and a father often away on business, someone was bound to get lost in the shuffle. Often it was Shane.

When he was about seven, my mother realized she wasn't quite as diligent with him as she'd been with the other boys. So she sat him down for an elementary school version of a heart-to-heart.

She started with some pretty powerful words. "Shane, I am sorry. I led you to believe you were allowed to behave like this, and it isn't true. From now on you will no longer get away with misbehaving."

He probably mumbled something or rolled his seven-year-old eyeballs. Who wouldn't, right? I was too little to remember his response, but since I've known at least one human child in my lifetime, and they are basically the same underneath it all, I can confidently say he took Mom's words as a challenge. He called her bluff. Or at least he tried to. Only she wasn't bluffing. She did a total reset with him beginning with an apology for not being more consistent. And then she treated him the age of whichever behavior he displayed.

If he acted like a seven-year-old, she let him do seven-year-old things like play with friends and walk by himself in the grocery store. When he acted like a four-year-old, he sat in the cart or walked with his hand in hers. He lost privileges, and she retaught her expectations in three-minute increments if necessary. She didn't care who judged her parenting. She didn't care if we were late or never showed up somewhere. Dinner could wait. Bedtime could wait. And maybe we would all just sit and wait until my brother knew she was in charge and her new boundaries were forever. He started off strong, but she was stronger. She had prayer on her side, which is basically like being handed the parenting tool of the world.

God is the God of do-overs. He loves a clean slate. If you haven't done it exactly like you've always wanted to do it, change it. Start with an apology and then reteach proper boundaries. Start today and determine to no longer hand over your parenting powers. Decide what sort of mother you want to be, and also keep in mind the kind of mom you don't want to mimic.

Are You Hagar or Sarai? (Feel Free to Say "Neither!")

Genesis 12 speaks of Abraham—a man so vital to biblical history that God calls himself "the God of Abraham." Abraham is central to our whole story. His faith is great enough that God makes a covenant with him back when his name is still Abram, which means "exalted father."

But Abram *isn't* a father—not yet. He and his wife, Sarai, are blessed exponentially by God, except where they both want God's blessing the most. Their deepest desire is to have a baby. An heir to whom they can pass along all their other blessings.

> My favorite motto is "carpe diem"—seize the day! You never know what tomorrow may bring so I try to live each day to its maximum potential. —Lauren, Missionary Mom of two

Abram's heart is heavy for his wife. For himself. For his household. He takes his devastation to God: "You have given me no descendants of my own, so one of my servants will be my heir" (Gen. 15:3). God clearly replies, "No, your servant will not be your heir, for you will have a son of your own who will be your heir" (v. 4).

God seals this deal through a call to action and a vision. Abram brings the sacrificial animals God asks for, and then God brings supernatural fire to move among the sacrifice in the form of a smoking pot and flaming torch. The Lord repeats his promise to Abram about his descendants and the vast land they will possess in God's mighty name.

Like so many of us, Abram and Sarai wait and wait and wait some more for these promises to manifest. In the face of God's own promises, at the end of God's blessed assurance that Abram will not depend upon a servant to be his heir, Sarai makes a decision for her household and the lives of generations to come. She accuses God and throws in the towel over a fight God never once asked her to take on as her own. "The Lord has prevented me from having children," she tells Abram. "Go and sleep with my servant. Perhaps I can have children through her" (Gen. 16:2).

This is a false accusation—she's grasping at straws and trying to put what she feels are logical steps to complete the promises God gave to her husband. Sarai takes her role as wife to a godly man and mother of a pending nation—a people foretold to be more numerous than the stars in the sky—and hands it over to her servant, Hagar . . . who of course becomes pregnant.

God's redemption of Sarai is a great story. But just as amazing is the quickly interjected story of Hagar. A servant to Sarai, likely with little choice about how she is to serve. They command; she obeys.

But a power shift takes place between the two women as Sarai hands over her rights as wife and leader of her household. Hagar sees herself in a new, false light. She decides her ability to become pregnant places her in a more prominent role than the mistress of the house, and she begins to show contempt toward Sarai. She forgets herself. She forgets who God has called her to be: an obedient servant, honoring others.

In true soap opera fashion, Sarai can't stomach it for another minute. Old habits die hard; again she turns and throws out harsh accusations to Abram. "This is all your fault!" (Gen. 16:5).

This lady has some issues.

Truly, none of these players are in God's will, so terrible choices beget horrible next steps as Abram throws his hands up in exasperated-husband surrender. And Sarai, rather than seeking forgiveness for setting Hagar up to fail and for disobeying God's directive, treats Hagar so badly that Hagar runs away.

But God is the God of reckoning. His whole desire for all his people is reconciliation—to each other, to him, to his original plan for relationship. He takes the messes we make, even the blatant ones that go directly opposite of what he promises us, and he makes them good. No, not just good. He turns them into something miraculous and steeped in a grace we could never deserve, let alone define with our limited human words.

He sends an angel to meet Hagar in the wilderness: "Hagar, Sarai's servant, where have you come from, and where are you going?" (Gen. 16:8). Then he gives her a directive many of us would continue running from: "Return to your mistress, and submit to her authority" (v. 9). Ouch.

But his instructions are not without the promise of blessing. He says do this and then I will bless you. Obey first and then you will receive. Order exists here—just as it should have throughout this whole story.

This same cause-and-effect is supposed to exist in our stories as well. But it gets lost when we look at our home lives and assume we know better than God our Father. We hand over power to others, and we get in the way of God's call on our children. We hand over our entire household. Sometimes our choices reap consequences that affect our kids their whole lives.

Hagar went on to have a son. Ishmael became Abram's firstborn heir—and an ongoing disruption in their once mostly peaceful home. Because God does more than we ever expect, he blessed Ishmael and Hagar, but their loss was incredible as well. Their road was riddled with struggle. As for Sarai, I imagine she never regretted anything more in her life than the day she handed over her God-given place as wife and mother. Let's be diligent today to maintain these roles in our own children's lives. If you've turned your children over to another, or to seemingly nothing, take them back.

It's never nothing. If you don't parent your children intentionally, the world will. The devil is eager to step in, in fact.

God has the perfect plan for our families, whether having children comes easily for you or you struggle with infertility or loss. Whether your family has baggage hanging from every shoulder. Whether you have children from previous relationships or a spouse who strays in marriage and returns with a new child. God can handle any of it if you'll let him. Let God lead the way back. Listen and submit to God's authority, never taking your role lightly. Decide who you are as a Missionary

Mom, and then be that mother in the face of every hard thing that comes your way. Be the one who remains focused on the task at hand, and just watch what your Father in heaven will do for you and your children forever.

Notes

1. John Gill, "Mark 14:8," *John Gill's Exposition of the Bible*, Bible Study Tools, accessed July 30, 2018, https://www.biblestudytools .com/commentaries/gills-exposition-of-the-bible/mark-14-8 .html.
2. Robert Burns, "To A Mouse, on Turning Her Up in Her Nest with the Plough," *Poems and Songs* (Mineola, NY: Dover, 1991), 33.
3. "Bible Timeline," Bible Hub, accessed July 30, 2018, http:// biblehub.com/timeline/esther/1.htm.
4. Gilda Radner, *It's Always Something* (New York: Simon and Schuster, 1989), 254–55.
5. Neel Burton, "These Are the 7 Types of Love," *Psychology Today*, June 25, 2016, https://www.psychologytoday.com/blog/hide-and -seek/201606/these-are-the-7-types-love.
6. David Livermore, *Cultural Intelligence: Improving Your CQ to Engage Our Multicultural World* (Grand Rapids: Baker Academic, 2009), 37.
7. All podcast quotes in this section are taken from Cindy Berglund, Stephanie Armstrong, and Laura Ludvigson, interview by Susie Larson, "The Power of a Mentor," *Faith Radio*, April 22, 2016, http://myfaithradio.com/2016/power-mentor.
8. "Generational Breakdown: Info About All of the Generations," The Center for Generational Kinetics, accessed July 30, 2018, http://genhq.com/faq-info-about-generations.

About the Author

$\mathcal{S}$hontell Brewer is a writer on her blog, *Nonsense At Its Finest*. By day she works as a classroom teacher, and weekends are mostly spent as an advocate for the steadily growing anti-trafficking movement in Nevada. As a licensed pastor with Foursquare International Church, she speaks around the country to youth, mothers, and churches. A wife for over twenty years, she and her husband have spent most of that time raising five kids. Together the family runs a monthly outreach in their home: a come-as-you-are dinner called Taco Tuesday. Shontell holds a bachelor's degree in education, a master's degree in teaching English as a second language, and an additional master's degree in Christian studies with an emphasis in urban ministry. Keep up with her day-to-day nonsense, books, and speaking engagements on Instagram @shontellbrewer.